Consecration to Jesus through St. Joseph

An Integrated Look At the Holy Family

Dr. Gregory Bottaro & Jennifer Settle

D1364986

CatholicPsych
PRESS

To Saint John Paul II, a model of
fatherhood who handed on the faith and
showed us what fatherhood looks like in
the example of Saint Joseph.

TABLE OF CONTENTS

FOREWORD

I had no idea that Saint Joseph would play such a pivotal role in my journey toward healing and how he would become a real father to me. You see, until I was in my 30s and met a Benedictine priest who loved Saint Joseph, I didn't give Saint Joseph much thought. I sort of just lumped him into "the Holy Family." I wasn't drawn to him in my prayer - that focused mostly on Jesus. It wasn't until I was encouraged by this Benedictine monk to open my heart to Saint Joseph and saw how this monk embodied the heart of Saint Joseph, that I came to see Saint Joseph as a real man, as a humble husband, and a gentle father - my father.

Along my path of healing, I began to turn to Our Lady and Saint Joseph as my parents. I began to share with them the joys and sorrows of my past. They showed me their parental love for me in those situations that wounded me or in the events of my past that brought me joy. Our Lady and Saint Joseph helped me to understand my identity as a beloved daughter of the Father through their parental love for me. I became their daughter and they became the source of parental love when I needed it. In particular, Saint Joseph became a real father to me. He became a father who was present in my life, one whom I could share my daughter's heart with, without fear of how he would receive me. His masculine, fatherly love has been such a source of healing for my feminine, daughter's heart.

As I grew to love and had encounters with the hearts of each of the Holy Family, I very much felt part of this family. The morning I was becoming a bride of Christ, as a Consecrated Virgin, I was in prayer with my spiritual director. As we prayed together, I very much felt the presence of the Holy Family. At that moment, I came to realize that for years I had seen myself as an "adopted" daughter of Our Lady and Saint Joseph, but in a few short hours,

I was becoming a bride of their son. Through my vocation, I was uniquely becoming a real part of the Holy Family for all eternity!

Along this journey, I discovered how much Dr. Greg and I shared a love and devotion to Saint Joseph! We both deeply desired more people to have a devotion to him and to receive him into their lives. What a gift to have that shared desire come to fruition through this Saint Joseph Consecration!

As you enter into this Consecration to Jesus through Saint Joseph, my hope for you is that you would encounter the heart of Saint Joseph in a profound and new way. My prayer for you is that you would open your heart to all he desires to share with you and trust in his fatherly presence in your life. May this consecration be a journey of healing, intimacy, and joy.

Saint Joseph, pray for us!

~ Jen Settle

INTRODUCTION

We need help. Our culture has been on a path of self-destruction for decades, and despite the warnings from many modern-day prophets, the trajectory has not changed. Our hope, of course, is in the Lord, who made heaven and earth and is with us until the end. However, these events unfold in a mysterious way in the context of history, and we are given powerful intercession and aid as a part of the arrangement.

Saint Joseph has been the silent protector of the Church since the beginning, but it is time to call out for him loudly. This devotional work is one simple and humble form of that initiative.

There are many forms of consecration, some of which you may have already taken part in. Consecrations are a form of devotion to help us grow closer to God. Through a consecration, we give God permission to take over our lives. He stands at the door and knocks, and this is one way of letting Him in.

The quickest and easiest way to grow is to follow a path that lines up with our humanity. Too many programs for growth either prioritize the spiritual over the material, or the material over the spiritual. Well-intentioned leaders can end up misleading their audience when they provide some plan of growth that doesn't actually respect the body-spirit nature of humanity.

We've tried to present a devotional exercise here that brings into focus the spiritual as well as psychological realities of being human. The psychological straddles the line of spiritual and physical - since it concerns the mind, which is an integration of our physical bodies and our spiritual life. We reflect on the full humanity of Saint Joseph, Our Lady, and Jesus to hopefully spark insights into what their humanity means for ours. In this way we hope to enter more fully, more perfectly, into the grace of our own Baptism.

What makes it integrated is the full participation on your part. If you want to consecrate yourself fully, with your body, mind, and spirit, do more than just form your intellect with the reflections. Let your spirit be moved by prayer and let your mind be moved with the journal prompts. Carve out the time you need to go deep into the reflections and explore what is moved within you, as unique son or daughter of God. This book provides a vehicle of grace, but you have to do your part to open up to it.

HOW TO USE THIS DEVOTIONAL

It is suggested to pick a feast day that is meaningful to you, or whichever one is more than 44 days away, and count back from there 44 days (6 weeks + 2 days). Not all specific dates are listed, since some feasts fall on different days each year, but you can easily count 6 weeks + 2 days back from the next feast day that you want to end on to make your consecration.

Each of the six weeks in the preparation has a specific theme, and its own set of prayers to be prayed after the reflection for the day. The prayers are found at the end of the week of reflections.

It is highly recommended to fully enter into this practice by responding each day to the journal prompts. Lined pages have been added for your convenience. This is a personal journal as much as a devotional. For this reason, you may want to have a few copies to repeat the practice yourself at different times of the year, or to give them away.

The question is often asked about starting over if a day or two is missed. We encourage you to keep up the best you can, but should a day get missed, catching up on the reflection for the day and the journal prompt should be enough to still derive the spiritual benefit of this devotion.

Saint Joseph has incredible power to transform your life if you let him. You are worth it. By picking this up you've already taken a step that is clearly in God's plan for you. Go all the way with it. Hold nothing back of yourself. Practically speaking, make a daily plan for how you are going to participate in this devotional.

You may have to make certain sacrifices for the next 44 days. You may have to wake up a little earlier or commit yourself to an activity like journaling that you've never really done before. Making this commitment to yourself, to Saint Joseph, and to God is a powerful way to hold nothing back of yourself from God. I promise you the graces returned to you will be countless.

It will be even more effective for you if you do this with someone else. Find someone else you are close to who will journey through this with you – someone you can share your responses with as well as your highs and lows throughout the 44 days. There is a Facebook group called "Saint Joseph Consecration" for everyone going through the Preparation. We often repeat the devotion as a group with emailed reflections as well. Make this a regular part of your life and share it with others.

Lastly, expect great things from God. He is never outdone in generosity. Of course, you should also expect pushback from the enemy, and don't be surprised if you go through some periods of desolation while practicing this devotion. The Immaculate, Chaste, and Sacred Hearts of the Holy Family will reign triumphant in your life though, and you can expect victory with confidence.

CALENDAR OPTIONS FOR MAKING YOUR CONSECRATION

January	Baptism of our Lord Jesus Christ*
February 2	Presentation of our Lord
March 19	Solemnity of St. Joseph
May 1	Feast of St. Joseph the Worker
June 28	Sacred Heart of Jesus
August 15	Assumption of Our Lady
September 8	Birth of Our Lady
October 22	Feast of St. John Paul II
November 1	All Saints Day
November	Solemnity of Christ the King*
December 25	Nativity of Jesus Christ
December	Feast of the Holy Family*

*moveable feasts

\\ WEEK 1 \\ KNOWLEDGE OF SELF
DAY 1: OUR IDENTITY AS A CHILD OF THE FATHER

The ultimate fulfillment of our life is union with God. We are made in God's image (where we come from) and we are made for union with Him (our fulfillment). As Saint Augustine says, "Our hearts are restless until they rest in you." What is it then, for our hearts to rest in God? It is our ultimate fulfillment. It is what we are made for, and we are ultimately unsatisfied and unhappy without it.

All human suffering and discontent can be summed up as an experience of not being in union with God. The cure for all human suffering and discontent is union with God. Therefore, it stands to reason that union with God should be the only principal goal we pursue.

We know that because of original sin, we lost the inheritance of union with God, but then Christ's Resurrection restored us to that inheritance. Jesus is the way. Through him, with him, and in him we can attain our ultimate fulfillment of union with God.

Our adopted sonship of the Father occurs through our union with Christ. This is everything. We enter into union with Christ through our Baptism. This sacrament initiates us into the greatest mystery of our human experience. In Baptism, we are united to Christ and receive all that is his. The end of this gift is union with the Father as Christ is one with the Father. This is a process though, and we don't get there all at once.

The journey towards union with God is the story of our own human development. God initiates and invites us into this journey, and then accompanies us along the way and provides everything that we need to keep going. Through Christ, he unites to our humanity, and our humanity can return to Him through Christ. This means we enter fully into God through the door of the humanity of Christ.

We draw our attention to the humanity of Christ to understand ourselves. We cannot hope to develop our humanity in some way differently than Christ developed his, and so we humble ourselves to accept the shocking mystery of God's humility in his Incarnation. God was a helpless baby and developed into the perfection of his humanity by means of a mother and father in the poor and humble circumstances of Nazareth.

Reflection Questions:
Who do you really see yourself as? If you were the child of a rich president, or a celebrity superstar, you would probably carry yourself with an attitude of being untouchable, like nothing could bother you. You'd live without a worry because you would know that everything will be taken care of for you. Who is your actual father? What kind of disposition should you walk around with? How does this compare to the disposition that you typically carry yourself with in your day-to-day emotional life?

I see myself as a middle class guy from a broken home and a "non-superstar" father. I'm trying to make the most of the opportunities that I've been given including the grace of my baptism, my current dating opportunity, and my intellectual and academic gifts. I fear that I won't reach my potential and lack the masculine strength/composure necessary to succeed.

\\ WEEK 1 \\ KNOWLEDGE OF SELF
DAY 2: THE ROLE OF JOSEPH AND MARY IN OUR LIVES

The family is often referred to as the *Schola Amoris*, or "School of Love," by the Church. Our families of origin are the places in which we are taught how to love. The foundation of this school is how we are first loved by our parents, and this love forms our identity and our tendencies of how we love.

The first lesson of love is instituted by the very marriage itself between our parents. The extent to which their marriage is based on an understanding of love-as-self-gift will more or less model for the children of the family what love is supposed to look like. This is where boys and girls witness what men and women are meant to be for each other. The second lesson of love is taught by the individual dynamics of each parent with each child. The child learns something of his or her own identity by the way he or she is loved by mom and dad. The love of a mother forms a particular part of our personality, and the love of a father forms another particular part of our personality.Our first educators would ideally be perfect. Unfortunately, each one of us suffers from concupiscence and imperfection. Our parents' imperfections turn into our own miseducation in the school of love. There are hundreds of ways that parents can provide imperfect love. Whenever a parent puts his or her own feelings and needs before the child's, a lesson of imperfect love is being taught. When a parent selfishly neglects a child's needs for nurturance, imperfect love is taught. When a parent selfishly neglects a child's needs for autonomy, imperfect love is also taught. There are too many ways to list that parents love imperfectly, but we've all received it in some form and measure. We all love imperfectly, but this has the most destructive influence on children who are made to learn what love *is* from their parents.

As we continue to reflect on the humanity of Jesus, we realize thathe was educated in the perfect school of love. His heart was formed in the dynamics of relationship with a perfect mom and a perfect dad. Jesus grew "in wisdom and in stature, and in favor with God and man" *(Lk 2:52)* within the Holy Family. This development was not only spiritual, it was human. His spiritual development was intimately tied to his human development as a boy learning how to first walk and talk, then pray, and participate in the normal activities of simple family life. He learned how to love his mom and dad, and others in the community, from the love Joseph and Mary shared with each other and with him. By God's design, his perfection was tied to the perfection of his formation in the perfect school of love at Nazareth, founded on Joseph's perfect fatherhood and Mary's perfect motherhood.

In our baptism we receive all that belongs to Jesus. His heart replaces our heart. His perfection replaces our wounds. All the areas of woundedness and imperfection within our hearts are healed through the grace of Baptism and the gradual transformation into union with Christ. Again, this is not merely a spiritual reality. The human reality of our spiritual development requires our human wounds and imperfections to be healed by the human perfection of the heart of Jesus. This is possible through our Baptism!

Through your Baptism, Jesus heals your mom-wounds and dad-wounds with his heart, which contains within it the perfection of a relationship with a perfect mom and a perfect dad. We begin reflecting on these wounds and imperfections here so that they may be present to the healing grace of a relationship with Mary and Joseph throughout this preparation.

Reflection Questions:
What are the areas of miseducation you may have received from your childhood? How might your parents' marriage have missed the mark of perfection in teaching you what love looks like? How might your relationship with your mom and with your dad missed the mark? What specific mom-wounds and dad-wounds do you need healed?

There are a lot of wounds from my childhood & relationship with/between my parents. Both of my parents frequently put their own feelings above my own. They did this by yelling a lot, often calling me disrespectful/disobedient, and failing to regulate their emotions, let alone regulating mine. Both of my parents

13

were unfaithful and failed to model spousal love for us.

KEY INSIGHT — loving your spouse is an essential way to love your children. Your children learn from the dynamics between the parents and internalize any friction / relational vice. Attack against mother = attack against self. Mother's pain/ weakness directly leads to less care for you. If parents are bad, what does that make you? Strong parents = strong self-image.

"Creatures are not born with desires unless satisfaction for these desires exists. A baby feels hunger; well, there is such a thing as food. A duckling wants to swim; well, there is such a thing as water. Men feel sexual desire; well, there is such a thing as sex. If I find in myself a desire which no experience in this world can satisfy, the most probable explanation is that I was made for another world."
~ C.S. Lewis, Mere Christianity

"If we consider the unblushing promises of reward and the staggering nature of the rewards promised in the Gospels, it would seem that Our Lord finds our desires not too strong, but too weak. We are half-hearted creatures, fooling about with drink and sex and ambition when infinite joy is offered us, like an ignorant child who wants to go on making mud pies in a slum because he cannot imagine what is meant by the offer of a holiday at the sea. We are far too easily pleased." ~ C.S. Lewis, The Weight of Glory

"The truth is that only in the mystery of the incarnate Word does the mystery of man take on light. For Adam, the first man, was a figure of Him Who was to come, namely Christ the Lord. Christ, the final Adam, by the revelation of the mystery of the Father and His love, fully reveals man to man himself and makes his supreme calling clear. It is not surprising, then, that in Him all the aforementioned truths find their root and attain their crown."
~ Gaudium et Spes 22

———

Jesus, the perfect human being, reveals to us our greatest capacity. In Jesus we find an insatiable thirst for souls. He gives himself to us completely, fully, pouring himself out for us to the last drop of his life so that we may have eternal happiness in Heaven. He died for us that we may be restored to a life we don't even clearly realize we lost. This is the model that teaches us what we are capable of: infinite love and insatiable thirst.

We may get a sense every once in a while of the infinite chasm of desire that exists within us. It is too terrifying to dwell in for very long, but we are certainly familiar with the lack of having enough. We seek our satisfaction in human love or things of this world, but feel like we are falling short all too often. We then blame ourselves or our loved ones for this emptiness.

Instead, let us consider the possibility that this lack of fulfillment may be God's way of teaching us that we are made for more. Instead of looking in this world for finite things to satisfy our longing for infinite things, let's turn our hearts to the infinite with the hope of our deepest desire being fulfilled.

We will revisit the celibacy of Saint Joseph at more depth later, but for now consider this: Jesus saw in his parents as he grew up the greatest human love possible between a husband and a wife, wrapped into the life of celibacy at the same time. The celibate marital love of Mary and Joseph formed Jesus to understand how our insatiable thirst could be directed beyond this world. This is not to say there is something wrong with sexual marital love, but there is something missing when we expect sexual love to satisfy our deepest longing. Only by submitting our vocational circumstances – whatever they are – under obedience to God will our circumstances become a means of reaching that deepest fulfillment.

Reflection Questions:
What joys has God blessed you with in your life? Did they leave you satisfied, and if so, for how long? What finite things of this world tempt you to find fulfillment in them? How far are you willing to go to imagine the joy you are actually created for?

Going to St. Mark's, making the basketball team, winning at debate, getting into Penn, Oxford, double major, becoming Catholic, Collegium, good friendships, Anita. Satisfaction at first, but every day I have to bring these gifts to fruition. Achievement is meaningless. It doesn't make me happy. What will durably make me happy will be heaven – becoming a saint.

I want my life to be pleasing to God. I want him to use my life, my gifts, my successes as an instrument of his grace. The center of my life is the Eucharist.

This sort of joy can only be realized through self-denial & total reliance/dependence on God. Accomplishments assure me of my abilities, but they offer transient joy. All earthly accomplishments are transient. See, Book of Wisdom.

Mary and Joseph were consecrated vessels of divine providence. Every ounce of Joseph's being was in service of his wife Mary and his child Jesus. Priestly fatherhood. Total gift of self.

I want to make a total gift of myself to God. Through me, God will accomplish his will in the world. God's plan for me is higher than my plan for myself. Submitting to his will for me will bring me everlasting joy and peace

17

"Now at the beginning of this pilgrimage, the faith of Mary meets the faith of Joseph. If Elizabeth said of the Redeemer's Mother, 'blessed is she who believed,' in a certain sense this blessedness can be referred to Joseph as well, since he responded positively to the word of God when it was communicated to him at the decisive moment. While it is true that Joseph did not respond to the angel's 'announcement' in the same way as Mary, he 'did as the angel of the Lord commanded him and took his wife.' What he did is the clearest 'obedience of faith'" (cf. Rom 1:5; 16:26; 2 Cor 10:5-6).

"One can say that what Joseph did united him in an altogether special way to the faith of Mary. He accepted as truth coming from God the very thing that she had already accepted at the Annunciation. The Council teaches: 'The obedience of faith must be given to God as he reveals himself. By this obedience of faith man freely commits himself entirely to God, making 'the full submission of his intellect and will to God who reveals,' and willingly assenting to the revelation given by him.' This statement, which touches the very essence of faith, is perfectly applicable to Joseph of Nazareth." ~ *Redemptoris Custos 4*

The first Adam was deceived by Lucifer, the fallen angel who had rebelled against God's plan. Lucifer doubted the goodness of God's plan and rejected him, then tempted Adam to the same path. In a sense, Lucifer gave birth to Adam's sinfulness.

If Christ is a new Adam and rescues humanity from the sin of the first Adam, it can be said that Joseph is a kind of reversal of the disobedience of Lucifer. Through Lucifer's disobedience, Adam's sin was born. Through Joseph's obedience, united to Our Lady's in marital union, Christ was born. Lucifer doubted the goodness of God, Joseph trusted in God's goodness. Lucifer rejected God's plan for humanity, Joseph accepted God's plan for humanity. Lucifer rebelled and took a third of God's angels from Heaven, Joseph submitted and ushered in salvation for all of humanity.

We are confronted daily with choices to trust the goodness of God or doubt Him and His plan. We are tempted to see things through the lens of our own perspective, limited here in space and time. We may know God's way in our hearts but think, "My way will be better this time."

No matter how many times we are wrong, our pride and egotism bring us back to this over and over again.We can choose to doubt like Lucifer or trust like Joseph.

Temptations may come to us in big things and in small. Someone wrongs us, and we are tempted to think it is better to hold onto our grudge instead of forgive. We suffer some imperfection in the silence of our heart, and we are tempted to think it is better to keep it hidden so as not to reveal our imperfections. God's way is to forgive. God's way calls us to reveal our imperfections and bring light to the darkness. Which way do we choose?

Others of us may be comfortable following God in the little ways but not in the big. We can forgive the driver who cuts us off, but what about the family member who cuts us out? We can reveal the bitterness against our spouse, but what about the lust? We can work on sacrificing our time for little things, but what about the most important things? What does your daily schedule look like? Your schedule reveals your priorities, and your priorities are based on your beliefs and who you trust.

In Saint Joseph we find the model of perfect trust and obedience. He had every reason to fear what lay before him, but he heard the message of the angel and trusted. He knew God's ways and he followed them. We know God's ways, we need Saint Joseph to help us follow them. We are invited to put everything on the line and radically trust that God is good, that He has a plan for us, and that following His ways will lead us along this path.

Reflection Questions:
What ways does the devil tempt us to doubt God's plan working in our life? What are we afraid of? What are our greatest temptations against faith?

We feel afraid to let things go. We feel afraid to take time off from a task to pray. We feel afraid to be ascetic and give things up. We feel afraid to take baby steps in pursuit of our goals. We are afraid that we will fail. We are afraid of sin rather than encouraged by the availability of sacraments and confident in God's mercy/providence.

We are afraid that our stumbling blocks will conquer us. We are afraid of embarrassment in the eyes of others. We are afraid of our faith being untrue and giving up on worldly pleasures for no reason. We are afraid of a life of grace being miserable/pleasureless/painful. We are afraid of foregoing success in the eyes of the world — being perceived as deluded or a failure.

If our sins overwhelm us and we can't live up to our own ideals, what does that say about us? I am afraid of proving to myself that I am fundamentally a sinner.

\\ WEEK 1 \\ KNOWLEDGE OF SELF
DAY 5: HOPE VS. DESPAIR

"Hope means hoping when things are hopeless, or it is no virtue at all... As long as matters are really hopeful, hope is mere flattery or platitude; it is only when everything is hopeless that hope begins to be a strength." ~ *G.K Chesterton*

"Guided by the Spirit, Simeon came into the temple; and when the parents brought in the child Jesus, to do for him what was customary under the law, Simeon took him in his arms and praised God, saying, 'Master, now you are dismissing your servant in peace, according to your word; for my eyes have seen your salvation, which you have prepared in the presence of all peoples, a light for revelation to the Gentiles and for glory to your people Israel.' And the child's father and mother were amazed at what was being said about him. Then Simeon blessed them and said to his mother Mary, 'This child is destined for the falling and the rising of many in Israel, and to be a sign that will be opposed so that the inner thoughts of many will be revealed—and a sword will pierce your own soul too.'" ~ *Lk2:25-35*

"My heart suffered with the Hearts of Jesus and Mary. Mine was a silent suffering, for it was my special vocation to hide and shield as long as God willed, the Virgin Mother and Son from the malice and hatred of men. The most painful of my sorrows was that I knew beforehand of their passion, yet would not be there to console them. Their future suffering was ever present to me and became my daily cross. I became, in union with my holy spouse, co-redemptor of the human race. Through compassion for the sufferings of Jesus and Mary I co-operated, as no other, in the salvation of the world." ~ *Saint Joseph's words in 1958 to Sister Mary Ephrem, during alleged apparitions from Our Lady of America and Saint Joseph (Promoted by Cardinal Burke).*

The entire witness of the Gospel is summed up in "Repent and **believe the good news.**" Jesus came to unite us to him through our humanity, and this was made possible given our sinful state through his conquering of death. He proclaims the existence of a Life after death. He comes to us to reveal the Kingdom of God, and he proves its existence by way of the empty tomb.

Trusting there is life after this world is the point to the whole story. This trust requires faith, and it sets us on a path of hope. We look forward to the next life with hope. Looking forward orients all that we say, think, and do while we are here in this world. It gives meaning to our actions, and meaning especially to our suffering.

To love is to be vulnerable to suffering. To love perfectly is to be vulnerable to the greatest suffering. We look at our Lady who held the dead body of her son, and we can't even imagine the pain of that suffering. Yet we also see in her example the witness of perfect hope.

Whatever suffering can be described of Christ in his passion and death, and our Blessed Mother who witnessed it first hand, can also be attributed to Saint Joseph, the protector of his wife and son. It was Saint Joseph's responsibility to protect his wife and child, as God lead him to do more than once in the Gospel. What suffering pierced his heart as he heard Simeon's prophecy of the sword that would pierce his wife's? If we reflect on the revelation of Christ's mission to his parents, we can only imagine what suffering befell Joseph as he anticipated what they would go through after he was gone and unable to protect them.

Fathers often experience a small share in this type of suffering when they are powerless against the suffering of their children or wife. This helpless powerlessness makes it abundantly clear that we are not ultimately in charge. The power of sickness and death reigns supreme in this world, ultimately winning over every person's effort to avoid it. We must all face this suffering, for ourselves and our loved ones, and make sense of it in light of God's promise.

In this we turn to Saint Joseph as a model of perfect faith, along with his wife who showed us to look past the grave. Whatever we suffer in this life, we, who have the benefit of knowing what happened three days later, can find consolation in the accompaniment of Joseph and Mary who suffered while maintaining hope.

Reflection Questions:
What attachments keep us from perfect hope? Attachments are not things we love, but the things we love without placing them in the context of God's plan. What specific relationships or desires do you need to purify? After writing these things out, place them in Saint Joseph's pure heart and ask him to reorient your love in the full light of God's plan.

We are attached to our comfort and daily patterns of living. We are attached to our contingent identities more than our Christian identities. We are attached to our wants — to apparent goods, which aren't real goods. My chief vices are lust and gossip.

\\ WEEK 1 \\ KNOWLEDGE OF SELF
DAY 6: LOVE VS. USE

"In the Liturgy, Mary is celebrated as 'united to Joseph, the just man, by a bond of marital and virginal love.' There are really two kinds of love here, both of which together represent the mystery of the Church - virgin and spouse - as symbolized in the marriage of Mary and Joseph. 'Virginity or celibacy for the sake of the Kingdom of God not only does not contradict the dignity of marriage but presupposes and confirms it. Marriage and virginity are two ways of expressing and living the one mystery of the Covenant of God with his people,' the Covenant which is a communion of love between God and human beings.

Through his complete self-sacrifice, Joseph expressed his generous love for the Mother of God, and gave her a husband's 'gift of self.' Even though he decided to draw back so as not to interfere in the plan of God which was coming to pass in Mary, Joseph obeyed the explicit command of the angel and took Mary into his home, while respecting the fact that she belonged exclusively to God."
~ *Redemptoris Custos, 20* We become one flesh, but I am entirely God's and God's alone, just as much as she is.

We are created with intense desire for intimate and infinite love. We are here in this world at first without a clear sense of how or where we are to find satisfaction of that desire. We then discover Christ and the Word of God, and are invited to follow him on a journey of faith and hope. It is daunting, exciting. What awaits is eternal life and union with God. LFG. Hero's journey
Without faith and hope, we are tempted to look for the satisfaction of our desires here and now. With faith and hope, we direct our longing to something bigger than what we see and feel in the here and now. Faith and hope, even if they require a sacrifice of immediate gratification, draw us out of ourselves and carry us beyond this time and place to where God exists. When we take matters into our own hands, we end up using those we are called to love. When we place ourselves in God's hands, we learn how to love.

To become like God - to be formed by Love, in the encounter with Love, into Love - is the greatest and most fulfilling reason to live. It is the meaning of life, and it is the only thing worth living for. As lofty and spiritual as this formation sounds, it is carried out in the simple circumstances of human lives. It is first experienced in the family.

We find a helpful model of this great mystery in the Holy Family, and especially in the life of Saint Joseph during this consecration.

Saint Joseph lived the mysterious combination of marriage plus the call to celibacy. This normal man loved perfectly and to the highest degree, both through the total renunciation of his own sexual gratification and physical fertility, but at the same time also with the marital relationship of self-gift oriented towards a particular woman. In this way, Joseph shows us the ultimate meaning of our body (to be a gift), and he also firmly establishes the possibility of living it out to its fullest within the context of married life (covenentally bound to one other person). In this greatest gift of self, the fertility he offers in his fatherhood is one that opens the door for the Incarnation, the birth of God himself in our world. What greater fertility than this could be imagined?

Saint John Paul II wrote, "Man and woman 'become a reciprocal gift through their masculinity and femininity, also through bodily union. Continence means a conscious and voluntary renunciation of this union and all that is connected with it" (*Theology of the Body* 77:3) ... "Yet, the celibate person 'has the awareness that in this way he can realize himself 'differently', and in some sense 'more' than in marriage, by becoming 'a sincere gift for others'" (*Theology of the Body* 77:2). Saint Joseph does both. He becomes the best version of himself, in some sense "more" than in the physical embrace of conjugal love, but realizes this sincere and total gift of self within the bond of marriage.

If we are faithful to the life God has called us to, we will not be left unsatisfied. We are afraid that if we don't grasp at our own satisfaction, we will never be satisfied. In all things, we can let go of our own needs and desires. Our Father loves us so much that

He is ready, willing, and able to provide for us everything that will actually fill our hearts. We have to trust Him, even if afraid, and follow Joseph's example. This is how we learn to truly love others.

Reflection Question:
What strings are attached to the love I give others?

We expect a reciprocal contribution to our lives. For example, I feel like I listen to my friends' problems & offer counsel when they need it, but my friends tune me out when I approach them with my problems. Now I see that in friendship presence/attunement are free gifts with no reciprocal expectation. Similarly, I attach strings to my love for Anita. I give her high importance in my life and expect her to open up to me / show vulnerability. Vulnerability is a gift. It can't be demanded/expected. I've got to be a hero and show up for her every day, the same way I have to show up for and love others.
I should place all my hopes of transcendent relational satisfaction/bliss in the domain of the infinite and eternal — union with God.

Mary's role in her virginal birth was to highlight the divine sonship of Jesus. Joseph, as her husband, was called to serve her in this role, and so also was called to highlight the divine sonship of his son. This is obviously not our particular role, yet we are all called to love one another with this kind of self-sacrifice. Even if we are not asked to live out celibacy within marriage, there are many ways that the teachings of Jesus through the Church challenge us in whatever state of life we are in. Joseph, who sacrificed his own physical sexuality for the good of his wife and God's plan for both of them can come to our aid to help us make the sacrifices of love that we are called to make.

Saint John Paul II said in one address, "The type of marriage to which the Holy Spirit led Mary and Joseph can only be understood in the context of the saving plan and of a lofty spirituality. The concrete realization of the mystery of the Incarnation called for a virgin birth which would highlight the divine sonship and, at the same time, for a family that could provide for the normal development of the Child's personality" *(Wednesday Audience, August 21, 1996).*

Once again, consider how Jesus was raised with the example of Mary and Joseph's love ever before him. His true humanity required true human development, and his personality formed in this school of love.

Our personalities develop also in the school of love. As we unite ourselves more deeply to Christ, spiritually through our Baptism and psychologically through our growth in faith, we can be perfected by the motherhood of Mary and the fatherhood of Joseph, in the perfect school of love of the Holy Family. Since our final destiny, the thing we are created for and the only thing worth living for is union with God, we need to learn how this happens in the context of our humanity, through our personalities. How we think about people, act towards people, and conduct ourselves both privately and publicly, and how we fundamentally relate to God facilitates our union with Him.

Jesus develops within us, as he developed in the little home of Nazareth. He grows, "in wisdom and in stature, and in favor with God and man" *(Lk 2:52)* in us and through us. This growth occurs under the watchful gaze and guidance of Mary and Joseph. They are our parents in the faith and they help us develop our Jesus-centered personalities.

Joseph is our father and gives us a perfect example that we can follow. Let us take Mary into our home as Joseph did, trusting in God's plan. Let's submit ourselves in silent prayer as Joseph did, in obedience to God's will. Let's make courageous decisions when prompted by the Spirit of God as Joseph did, even when they go against what we might feel like doing. Let's say yes to God, that Jesus may grow within us, and we may become the saints we are created to be.

Reflection Question:
What part of my personality have I let slide that is not in conformity with the saint God wants me to become?

_____

_____

_____

_____

_____

_____

_____

_____

_____

_____

_____

_____

_____

_____

First Prayer to St. Joseph

St. Joseph, whose protection is so great, so strong, so prompt before the throne of God, I place in you all my interest and desires.

St. Joseph, assist me by your powerful intercession, and obtain for me from your divine Son all spiritual blessings, through Jesus Christ, our Lord. So that, having engaged here below your heavenly power, I may offer my thanksgiving and homage to the most loving of Fathers.

St. Joseph, I never weary contemplating you, and Jesus asleep in your arms; Press Him close in my name and kiss His fine head for me and ask Him to return the kiss when I draw my dying breath. St. Joseph, patron of departing souls, pray for me. Amen.

Ave Maris Stella

Hail, Star of Ocean!
Portal of the sky,
Ever Virgin Mother,
Of the Lord most high.

Oh! by Gabriel's Ave,
Uttered long ago,
Eve's name reversing,
Establish peace below.

Break the captive's fetters;
Light on blindness pour;
All our ills expelling,
Every bliss implore.

Show yourself a mother;
Offer him our sighs,
Who for us Incarnate
Did not you despise.

Virgin of all virgins!
To your shelter take us;
Gentlest of the gentle!
Chaste and gentle make us.

Still as on we journey,
Help our weak endeavor,
Till with you and Jesus
We rejoice forever.

Through the highest heaven,
To the Almighty Three,
Father, Son, and Spirit,
One same glory be.

\\ Week 2 \\ Casting Off the Spirit of the World
Day 8: Vice of Pride and Virtue of Humility

Pride was the first sin committed. It is the root of the Original Sin. Adam and Eve believed the serpent's lie that God didn't want them to be like Him - when, in fact, they already were made in His image and likeness. They gave into pride by grasping for what they believed the Father desired to keep from them.

Pride is the summit of self-love. It is directly opposed to submission to God. Pride makes us unwilling to acknowledge dependence on God. It was pride that kept Lucifer, the Angel of Light, from submitting to God. He saw that the Son of God would become human through Our Lady and would be raised in a human family with Saint Joseph. He would not serve a God who would stoop to the level of humanity. He made a free and eternal choice to reject God.

Pride keeps us from acknowledging our weaknesses and poverty. In fact, pride encourages us to hide our poverty from the world, because pride sees poverty as unloveable. Pride encourages us to take personal credit for the gifts that God give us. It desires us to glorify ourselves and not the God who gave us such gifts. Pride tempts us to minimize our defects and magnify the defects of others.

The life of Saint Joseph is a witness to us of the virtue of humility which overcomes the vice of pride. In Father Raniero Cantalamessa's Advent retreat to Pope Francis and the Roman Curia in 2013, he defined the meaning of humility. "The word 'humility' has two fundamental meanings: one objective, which indicates in fact lowliness, littleness or poverty and one subjective, which indicates the feeling and recognition that one has of one's own littleness."

Let us contemplate the objective humility of Saint Joseph within the annunciation by the angel, after he had decided to quietly divorce Mary: "Such was his intention when, behold, the angel of the Lord appeared to him in a dream and said, 'Joseph, son of David, do not be afraid to take Mary your wife into your home. For it is through the holy Spirit that this child has been conceived in her.' ... When Joseph awoke, he did as the angel of the Lord had commanded him and took his wife into his home." *(Matthew 1:20, 24)* When Saint Joseph awoke from the dream, he humbly set aside his will to obey the will of God. "Instead of defending himself and demanding his rights, Joseph opts for a solution that represents an enormous sacrifice for him." *(Pope Francis homily December 23, 2013)* Unlike Lucifer, who was dominated by pride, Joseph made a free and humble choice to serve God.

"Joseph was a man who always listened to God's voice, profoundly sensitive to his hidden will, a man attentive to the messages that came to him from the depths of his heart and from above. He did not persist in pursuing his own plan for his life, he did not allow rancor to poison his soul, but was ready to place himself at the service of the thing that was presented to him in a disconcerting way" *(Pope Francis homily December 23, 2013)*. Saint Joseph's life is a witness to us of humble dependence, submission, and attachment to the Lord's will. Saint Joseph, teach us to be humble of heart.

Reflection Questions:
How does pride manifest in your life? Do you struggle to admit sin in the Sacrament of Confession? Do you envy others for gifts you don't possess or seek affirmation for your gifts? Are you willing to yield to the will of God for your life or do you seek only your will? Can you share one of your poverties with the Lord today?

_____
_____
_____
_____
_____
_____
_____
_____
_____

\\ WEEK 2 \\ CASTING OFF THE SPIRIT OF THE WORLD
DAY 9: VICE OF GREED AND VIRTUE OF GENEROSITY

"One gives freely, yet grows all the richer;
another withholds what he should give,
and only suffers want." *(Proverbs 11:24-25)*

To the outside world, Saint Joseph didn't possess much. He was a simple carpenter who provided very simply for his little family. He would have been "successful" according to the world if he focused on the material things. If he wanted to be successful, He should have had an occupation that provided more than what his family needed. He "should have" seen value in the things of the world. This is the language of greed - love and selfish desire for the material things, while being blinded to the value of spiritual things.

Little did the world know that inside the simple house of this simple carpenter lived the Immaculate and Sacred Hearts! Little did they know that God literally dwelt among them! Saint Joseph lived a life of generosity. He could have followed through on his decision to divorce Mary, but he freely chose to give his life to protect her and the Son of God. He lavished his love upon them. He protected Our Lady and the Son of God in such a hidden way that even his fellow villagers didn't know who Jesus was, "Is not this the carpenter's son? Is not his mother called Mary?" *(Matthew 13:55)*

Saint Joseph knew the treasure he possessed was the richest of all riches! Every day he labored to protect and care for Our Lady and Jesus. He generously gave all he had to keep them safe, until it was time for Jesus to begin his public ministry. He gave of himself to bring up Jesus in the Jewish faith and to teach him to understand the things of the world. Joseph taught Him that a generous heart overcomes greed and selfishness. This is a lesson Jesus may have remembered when Judas betrayed him for 20 silver pieces.

A heart disposed to greed closes itself to others. It demands that one keeps whatever it possesses for itself. It desires to take possession of what others possess. A generous heart, like the heart of Saint Joseph, opens itself and gives everything it possesses. It empties itself for the good of the other. "The less we have, the more we give. Seems absurd, but it's the logic of love." (Saint Theresa of Calcutta)

Reflection Questions:

Do you have a love of the things you possess or do you see all that you have generously given to you by the Lord? Are you selfish about your time, your attention, your money, or sharing what you have? How is your heart open to giving to others what the Lord has generously given to you? What are you holding back for yourself?

_____

_____

_____

_____

_____

_____

_____

_____

_____

_____

_____

_____

_____

_____

_____

_____

_____

_____

_____

_____

_____

_____

_____

\\ WEEK 2 \\ CASTING OFF THE SPIRIT OF THE WORLD
DAY 10: VICE OF ENVY AND VIRTUE OF LOVE

"Rid yourselves of all malice and all deceit, insincerity, envy, and all slander; like newborn infants, long for pure spiritual milk so that through it you may grow into salvation, for you have tasted that the Lord is good."
(1 Peter 2: 1-3)

In those moments when we wish we had the talent, relationship, financial success, or even holiness of another, our hearts become envious. We take on a posture of comparing our life to another's and wishing we had it, which means we wish that they didn't. We wish we could possess that which the other possesses. Envy destroys love.

Love wills the good of the other. Love finds joy when another is successful. To love another is to be willing to suffer for them. When someone we love is given gifts or graces, we celebrate with them. An envious heart is saddened at the supernatural gifts or graces that another has received from the Lord.

Saint Joseph lived and loved the Immaculate and Sacred Hearts. He knew them intimately. They possessed gifts and graces that Saint Joseph could never possess. He could never be the Son of God. He could never be Immaculately Conceived. He was at total peace with himself and the Father's confidence in his care for Our Lady and Jesus. Joseph lived a life of love. He longed to love them with his whole heart. He longed, not to possess or grasp for what they had, but to be a gift to them and to humbly receive what they desired to give him - their love. Joseph was not saddened by their gifts. He didn't compare himself to the mother of the Redeemer and the Son of God, because he would always come up short! He did, as Saint Mother Theresa of Calcutta wrote, "small things with great love."

To love others with this kind of disinterested love means that we first have to receive the love that God has for us. It is impossible to be at peace with the gifts that others possess unless we know what gifts we possess. The greatest gift we could ever have is the love of God. When we are grounded on this foundation, we can truly be happy for others and the gifts they received. When we are missing this foundation, we will constantly be looking at the gifts of others as things that could potentially give us value instead.

Reflection Questions:
Do you long for things that others possess? Do you compare yourself to others? Do you wish others didn't have the gifts and spiritual graces they do? Are you sad or joyful when a friend receives something you wish you had? Are you willing to suffer for the good of the other? Are you at peace with what the Father has given you?

\\ WEEK 2 \\ CASTING OFF THE SPIRIT OF THE WORLD
DAY 11: VICE OF ANGER AND VIRTUE OF KINDNESS

> "For gracious and merciful is he,
> slow to anger, rich in kindness,
> and relenting in punishment."
> *Joel 2:13*

The Father chose Saint Joseph to be the husband of Our Lady and the father of Jesus. The Father shaped Joseph's heart to be like His. He planted in the heart of Joseph the desire to care and provide for them and to love them with the heart of the Father. The Father's heart is "gracious and merciful.... slow to anger, rich in kindness." The heart of Saint Joseph was molded in these virtues. The way that he loved Our Lady and Jesus was from his kind and loving heart. As Saint Theresa of Calcutta once said, "Be the living expression of God's kindness." This was the heart of Joseph. He was the living expression of the kindness of God.

A misinterpretation of Saint Joseph is that when he learned of her pregnancy, he decided to "divorce her quietly," because he thought Our Lady had been with another man and conceived a child. Saint Joseph loved and knew the Immaculate Heart of Mary. He knew her vow to virginity. He knew she was incapable of such duplicity. Never did it enter his heart to be angry with Our Lady. He knew that she was carrying the Messiah. He knew he was not worthy to be the husband of the Mother of God, nor the father to the Son of God. The thought of being chosen to be the father of the Messiah and the husband of the Mother of God created doubt in the heart of Joseph that he was up for such a task. Was he man enough? Was he capable of bringing the Mother of the Son of God into his home and to care for her and the Messiah? In Joseph's heart, the "kindest" decision was to divorce her.

But the Father sends an angel to tell Joseph in a dream, "Joseph, son of David, do not be afraid to take Mary your wife into your home." *(Matthew 1:20)* From the Father's kind heart toward

Joseph, it is as if He says to him: "Do not be afraid, Joseph, I will give you everything you need to care for them. Your kind heart is like mine. You will love them as I do. I trust you with their protection." Scripture tells us that "When Joseph awoke, he did as the angel of the Lord had commanded him and took his wife into his home." *(Matthew 1: 24)*

As Our Lady was about to deliver Jesus, the kind heart of Joseph desired to protect Our Lady and the Son of God. His kindness to Our Lady provided her a place to rest and to deliver Jesus. In what must have been the most beautiful and humble moment in the life of Saint Joseph, he literally received the Messiah into the world as Our Lady delivered him. His father's heart was filled with joy that the Savior of the world had entered the world. What was the response of Herod's heart when he learned of the Savior's birth? "When Herod realized that he had been deceived by the magi, he became furious. He ordered the massacre of all the boys in Bethlehem and its vicinity two years old and under, in accordance with the time he had ascertained from the magi." *(Matthew 2:16)* He response was anger, which led to death. The kindness of Saint Joseph led to life! May our hearts be molded in the Father's heart - "gracious and merciful.... slow to anger, rich in kindness."

Reflection Questions:
Do you struggle with responding to frustrations or the unexpected with anger? How do you show kindness to those around you? In your family? Amongst your friends? Do you struggle with receiving the kindness of others? Do you show mercy and kindness to those who have wounded you or does your heart still harbor anger? Where anger still resides in your heart, let us open that place to the kindness of the Father and ask Saint Joseph's intercession for our healing.

\\ WEEK 2 \\ CASTING OFF THE SPIRIT OF THE WORLD
DAY 12: VICE OF LUST AND VIRTUE OF SELF-MASTERY

"'Joseph... took his wife; but he knew her not, until she had borne a son' *(Mt 1:24-25).* These words indicate another kind of closeness in marriage. The deep spiritual closeness arising from marital union and the interpersonal contact between man and woman have their definitive origin in the Spirit, the Giver of Life *(cf. Jn 6:63).* Joseph, in obedience to the Spirit, found in the Spirit the source of love, the conjugal love which he experienced as a man. And this love proved to be greater than this 'just man' could ever have expected within the limits of his human heart." *(Pope Saint John Paul II, Redemptoris Custos, 19)*

Read that last line again... "Joseph found in the Spirit the source of love, the conjugal love which he experienced as a man. And this love proved to be greater than this 'just man' could ever have expected within the limits of his human heart." Many artists depict Saint Joseph as a very old man (some even show him standing over Mary and Jesus at the Nativity using a cane!). Why, for centuries, have artists depicted him so? Were they uncomfortable thinking about a young, strong, and virile man marrying and living with the Virgin Mary? Were they what Pope Saint John Paul II called "masters of suspicion" in his *Theology of the Body* (someone who's heart cannot see purity and projects impurity onto others)?

Saint Joseph was a man. He was a man who possessed natural desires toward what is true, good, and beautiful. Besides God, himself, what is more true, good, and beautiful than the Virgin Mary? Day in and day out, Joseph was surrounded by perfect femininity, but more than that, he loved and was loved by perfect femininity! As a true man, Saint Joseph lived (maybe more than any other man) perfect self-mastery. Daily, he ordered his passions, his attractions to Our Lady toward love. He didn't "white knuckle" his chastity. He opened his desires to the Lord and was given grace to love Our Lady rightly, in all his masculinity. The perfect love of Joseph would never have desired to use her. He only desired to love her.

If Saint Joseph was so elderly, as some art portrays him, and he was no longer able to love passionately, then he wouldn't have been a man who lived the virtue of self-mastery. Self-mastery needs attraction and passion to order. The real Saint Joseph had these qualities, and he had them for Our Lady, as her husband, as a man would. It was in this experience of authentic masculinity that the true power of his self-mastery was opened to the world.

Reflection Questions:
"The virtuous man is he who freely practices the good." (*CCC 1804*) How freely do you practice the good of self-mastery? What keeps you from freely living a life of virtue? What are areas of your life that are in need of ordering? How has your understanding of the lived experience of Saint Joseph, man and husband, changed?

"To live well is nothing other than
to love God with all one's heart, with all one's soul
and with all one's efforts; from this it comes about that
love is kept whole and uncorrupted
(through temperance)."
~*St. Augustine*

The Lord desires us to find all that He created to be good and pleasurable. He has given us all good gifts to be received and used for our good. He did the same with Adam and Eve. He gave them the entire garden in which to find pleasure and sustenance. He only asked them not to eat of the fruit of the tree in the middle of the garden, the tree knowledge of good and evil. As we know, Adam and Eve believed the fruit of this tree was being kept from them, even though they had the entire garden to keep them satisfied. They grasped for more than what they needed and as a result, perfect love expired from their hearts.

"The woman saw that the tree was good for food and pleasing to the eyes, and the tree was desirable for gaining wisdom. So she took some of its fruit and ate it; and she also gave some to her husband, who was with her, and he ate it" *(Genesis 3: 6)*. Gluttony is a grasping. It is a taking of more than is needed. Gluttony is a disordered appetite, which abuses the legitimate pleasure God has attached to it. It weakens the will. It fosters laziness and impurity. Adam and Eve didn't trust that God had given them all they needed to be happy.

Our Lady undid the taking of Eve by her posture of receptivity before God. When the angel came to her to announce the Lord's desire for her to conceive the Son of God within her, she gave her fiat, her yes. She opened to receive the gift of the Holy Spirit and life was conceived within her. She trusted the Lord would provide all she needed, and that providence came through Saint Joseph.

Saint Joseph was a stabilizing force in the life of Our Lady and Jesus. He was their protector and guard, but he was also a source of great love. His chaste love for Our Lady was given in temperance. In knowing of Our Lady's witness of receptivity to the Holy Spirit, he never desired to grasp. He only desired to love her rightly. Temperance did not make his love cold. He loved Our Lady with real passion, but with passion that was ordered to her good (and to his). Temperance "moderates the attraction of pleasures and provides balance ... it ensures the will's mastery over instincts and keeps desires within the limits of what is honorable. The temperate person directs the sensitive appetites toward what is good..." (Catechism of the Catholic Church 1809)

Reflection Questions:
Do you find yourself unsatisfied with the things you have been given? Do you find yourself longing for more of something good? Are you tempted to grasp for more than what you have? How can the temperance of Saint Joseph - attraction to a good, but limited to what is honorable - be a witness of healthy balance in your life?

\\ WEEK 2 \\ CASTING OFF THE SPIRIT OF THE WORLD
DAY 14: VICE OF SLOTH AND VIRTUE OF ZEAL

The early Church Fathers called the vice of sloth, or acedia, the "noonday devil." It is reminiscent of that feeling at the midpoint of the day, when we grow sluggish and weary. Who can't relate to that? We become tempted to just "get through" whatever it is we are doing, to not give our best. The word acedia in English comes from the Latin, which itself comes from the Greek akèdia, meaning "lack of care." In the spiritual life, acedia makes us indifferent, discouraged, and apathetic to the will of God.

Joseph's life didn't go as he planned. He was a simple man, a simple carpenter who fell in love with a simple girl from Nazareth, and desired a simple life with her. He prepared a simple home for his bride and was excited to begin this simple life. In an instant of hearing the news from Mary, his life became anything but simple. Suddenly, he is faced with his virgin bride carrying the Messiah. He was faced with the reality of the shame and possible death she could endure, because she was with child. He was faced with knowing that he would be responsible for the protection and raising of the Son of God! In that instant, Joseph's plans went up in smoke.

If anyone had earned a "pity party," it was Joseph. The reality of his life turning out so radically different than he had dreamed and planned, could earn Joseph a momentary pause to adjust to his new reality. We could give Joseph the benefit of a little moment of hesitancy - wondering if he were up to such a task. If Joseph were prone to acedia, this news could have sent him down a path of a life that was too much to bear, a life of discouragement, a life ultimately indifferent to the things of God, a life fleeing from union with God. Throughout scripture, however, we see Joseph's life as a life of action.

"When Joseph awoke, he did as the angel of the Lord had commanded him and took his wife into his home." *(Matthew 1:24)*

"When they had departed, behold, the angel of the Lord appeared to Joseph in a dream and said, 'Rise, take the child and his mother, flee to Egypt, and stay there until I tell you. Herod is going to search for the child to destroy him.' Joseph rose and took the child and his mother by night and departed for Egypt." *(Matthew 2:13-14)*

"When Herod had died, behold, the angel of the Lord appeared in a dream to Joseph in Egypt and said, 'Rise, take the child and his mother and go to the land of Israel, for those who sought the child's life are dead.' He rose, took the child and his mother, and went to the land of Israel. But when he heard that Archelaus was ruling over Judea in place of his father Herod, he was afraid to go back there. And because he had been warned in a dream, he departed for the region of Galilee. He went and dwelt in a town called Nazareth, so that what had been spoken through the prophets might be fulfilled, "He shall be called a Nazorean." *(Matthew 2:19-23)*

Joseph was a man of action - a man filled with zeal. He had great energy and passion in pursuit of living out his identity as husband and father. Joseph was not indifferent to the will of God. He was moved with great love for the Lord, Our Lady, and Jesus. This was a passionate love - a heroic love of a man, a husband, and a father - that lead him to be willing to let go of his plans for a simple life and to embrace a willingness to risk his life to protect them. Joseph did not live a life lost of meaning, because the Lord's plan was different than his. With the Lord's encouragement, Joseph embraced his new life. It was an unexpected life of loving the Mother of God and the Son of God with a heart willing to sacrifice everything to care for them.

Reflection Questions:
Have you become discouraged with your life, your relationships, or your vocation when things don't seem to go the way you planned? How can you open yourself to the Lord's encouraging will for you? How can even the "action" of a life of prayer help you to overcome the apathy in your life?

WEEK 2 PRAYERS

Litany of the Holy Spirit
Lord, *have mercy on us.*
Christ, *have mercy on us.*
Lord, *have mercy on us.*

Father all-powerful, *have mercy on us.*
Jesus, Eternal Son of the Father, Redeemer of the world, *save us.*
Spirit of the Father and the Son, boundless life of both,
sanctify us.
Holy Trinity, *hear us.*

Holy Spirit, proceeding from the Father and the Son, *enter our hearts.*
Holy Spirit, equal to the Father and the Son, *enter our hearts.*

Promise of God the Father,	*have mercy on us.* (after each line)
Ray of heavenly light,	*have mercy on us.*
Author of all good,	...
Source of heavenly water	...

Consuming fire
Ardent charity
Spiritual unction
Spirit of love and truth
Spirit of wisdom and understanding
Spirit of counsel and fortitude
Spirit of knowledge and piety
Spirit of the fear of the Lord
Spirit of grace and prayer
Spirit of peace and meekness
Spirit of modesty and innocence
Holy Spirit, the Comforter
Holy Spirit, the Sanctifier
Holy Spirit, Who governs the Church
Gift of God, the Most High
Spirit Who fills the universe
Spirit of the adoption of the children of God

Holy Spirit, inspire us with horror of sin.
Holy Spirit, come and renew the face of the earth.
Holy Spirit, shed Thy light in our souls.
Holy Spirit, engrave Thy law in our hearts.
Holy Spirit, inflame us with the flame of Thy love.
Holy Spirit, open to us the treasures of Thy graces.
Holy Spirit, teach us to pray well.
Holy Spirit, enlighten us with Thy heavenly inspirations.
Holy Spirit, lead us in the way of salvation.
Holy Spirit, grant us the only necessary knowledge.
Holy Spirit, inspire in us the practice of good.
Holy Spirit, grant us the merits of all virtues.
Holy Spirit, make us persevere in justice.
Holy Spirit, be Thou our everlasting reward.

Lamb of God, Who takes away the sins of the world,
Send us Thy Holy Spirit.
Lamb of God, Who takes away the sins of the world,
pour down into our souls the gifts of the Holy Spirit.
Lamb of God, Who takes away the sins of the world,
grant us the Spirit of wisdom and piety.

V. Come, Holy Spirit! Fill the hearts of Thy faithful,
R. And enkindle in them the fire of Thy love.

Let us pray. Grant, O merciful Father, that your Divine Spirit
may enlighten, inflame and purify us, that He may penetrate
us with His heavenly dew and make us fruitful in good works,
through Our Lord Jesus Christ, Your Son, Who with You, in the
unity of the same Spirit, lives and reigns, one God, forever and
ever. Amen.

Litany of Humility

O Jesus! Meek and humble of heart, hear me.

From the desire of being esteemed, deliver me Jesus

From the desire of being loved, deliver me Jesus

From the desire of being extolled, deliver me Jesus

From the desire of being honored, deliver me Jesus

From the desire of being praised, deliver me Jesus

From the desire of being preferred, deliver me Jesus

From the desire of being consulted, deliver me Jesus

From the desire of being approved, deliver me Jesus.

From the fear of being humiliated, deliver me Jesus

From the fear of being despised, deliver me Jesus

From the fear of suffering rebukes, deliver me Jesus

From the fear of being calumniated, deliver me Jesus

From the fear of being forgotten, deliver me Jesus

From the fear of being ridiculed, deliver me Jesus

From the fear of being wronged, deliver me Jesus

From the fear of being suspected, deliver me Jesus

That others may be loved more than I, Jesus, grant me the grace to desire it.

That others may be esteemed more than I, Jesus, grant me the grace to desire it

That in the opinion of the world, others may increase and I may decrease, Jesus, grant me the grace to desire it.

That others may be chosen and I set aside, Jesus, grant me the grace to desire it.

That others may be praised and I unnoticed, Jesus, grant me the grace to desire it.

That others may be preferred to me in everything, Jesus, grant me the grace to desire it.

That others become holier than I, provided that I may become as holy as I should, Jesus, grant me the grace to desire it. Amen.

\\ WEEK 3 \\ KNOWLEDGE OF THE BLESSED VIRGIN MARY
DAY 15: DEVOTION TO MARY

Joseph was the first to consecrate himself to Jesus through Our Lady. His life and devotion to Our Lady is the model for us of how we are called to give everything to Jesus through Mary. Joseph gave over his whole life to his Holy Family. Our Lady was a witness to Joseph of how to have deep trust in the Lord and to be a total gift of self when she gave her fiat at the Annunciation. Our Lady, in her femininity, was the one to show him what it meant to be open and receptive before the Lord.

"Holy women are an incarnation of the feminine ideal; they are also a model for all Christians, an example of how the Bride must respond with love to the love of the Bridegroom." *(Pope John Paul II, Mulieris Dignitatem)*

By her witness and her femininity, she lovingly schooled Joseph on how to open every part of his life and heart to Jesus. He watched Our Lady give everything to Jesus. He saw her give life to Jesus in the stable in Bethlehem and nourish the Son of God at her breast. He saw her pouring out her whole life for Jesus.

Even before the Annunciation or the birth of Jesus, Our Lady was a witness to Joseph of total devotion to the Lord. Our Lady came to Joseph before they were married to tell him of her desire to be consecrated to the Lord - to give the total gift of herself to the Lord through her vow to perpetual virginity. Obviously, it would be something in which Joseph would also need to give his fiat. She told Joseph of her fiat to the Lord - before she gave it at the Annunciation. Agreeing to a life of virginity, Our Lady and Saint Joseph were united in their love for the Lord and for each other.

After the Annunciation and birth of Jesus, they were both devoted to Him. Their marriage and their life revolved around the protection and care for Him. As a young boy, Jesus would have seen Joseph's devotion to Our Lady. Every decision he made in his life revolved around Our Lady and Jesus. Joseph modeled for Jesus - and he still models for all of us - what true devotion to Jesus through Our Lady looks like - a free, total, faithful, and fruitful love.

Joseph gave his free yes to Our Lady to love and care for her. He held nothing back from them - he gave a total gift of himself to them. He never strayed from his love and care for them. To his death, he remained faithful to them and to the promise he made to the Father to care for them. His love and devotion to Jesus and Our Lady was fruitful. Through his protection and spousal love for Our Lady and his fatherly love for Jesus, he participated in the salvation of the whole world. It is because of the Lord's providence in gifting Joseph with a deep love and devotion to Jesus through Our Lady that, years later, the Son of God would die on a cross for us in obedience to His heavenly Father. Devotion to Saint Joseph is devotion to Jesus through Mary.

Reflection Questions:
Are there people in your life who have given witness to you of the Father's love and devotion? Have you ever shared with any of them how much their witness meant to you? Are you beginning to see how a devotion to Saint Joseph will lead you to deeper devotion to Jesus and Our Lady?

_____
_____
_____
_____
_____
_____
_____
_____
_____
_____
_____
_____
_____
_____

\\ Week 3 \\ Knowledge of the Blessed Virgin Mary
Day 16: Immaculate Conception

> "'God sent forth his Son', but to prepare a
> body for him, he wanted the free co-operation of a
> creature. For this, from all eternity God chose for the
> mother of his Son a daughter of Israel, a young Jewish
> woman of Nazareth in Galilee, 'a virgin betrothed to a
> man whose name was Joseph, of the house of David;
> and the virgin's name was Mary'."
> *(Catechism of the Catholic Church, 488)*

"From all eternity God chose for the mother of his Son a daughter of Israel." We all know the difference between the feeling of being chosen and not being chosen. When we are chosen, whether for a job, in marriage, for priesthood, or even in dodgeball, what wells up inside of us is that someone saw something in us that was of value to them. They saw our goodness and our worth and chose us. When we are overlooked for someone else, we feel less than. We feel like we didn't "measure up" to what they were looking for.

From all eternity Mary was called by God to be the mother of His Son. Her chosen-ness came through her Immaculate Conception.

"As for Our Lady, the most holy Virgin, she was conceived in the usual way of generation. But since in His plan God has predestined her from all eternity to be His Mother, He kept her pure and free from all stain, although by her nature she could have sinned" *(St. Francis de Sales, Homily of December 8, 1622).*

As much as God chose Mary, he also chose Joseph. He made Mary Immaculate so she could not only give her immaculate DNA to the Son of God, but also that her womb could be "without spot or wrinkle or any such thing" *(Ephesians 5:27).* Her Immaculate womb was chosen to be the Ark to carry the Son of God. So often we've heard of Joseph was just a convenient necessity, because Mary needed a husband to protect her. What a disservice to Joseph!

As important as Mary's purity was to the Father, so was Joseph's virtue! This man was going to raise the Son of God. The Father desired this man to be just, kind, compassionate, loving, and a guardian of both Our Lady and Jesus. The Father would not entrust the care of His Son, or the Immaculate one, to just "any" man. Although Joseph was not immaculately conceived, the Father chose him, the just and righteous man. Even when Joseph felt the weight of being chosen for this task, deep down, he must have felt joy that the Father had seen his goodness and found him worthy.

Reflection Questions:
When have you experienced the suffering of not being chosen? How can you bring that to the Father and let Him remind you that He has already chosen you from all time? How can Our Lady and Saint Joseph share in that joy with you?

\\ Week 3 \\ Knowledge of the Blessed Virgin Mary
Day 17: Annunciations of Mary and Joseph

We don't often think that Saint Joseph played a role at the Annunciation. We know that Our Lady was alone when the Angel Gabriel approaches her to announce her being chosen to conceive and bear the Son of God, but was Joseph in Our Lady's heart when she gave her fiat, her yes?

"At the Annunciation, Our Lady also acted as the wife of Joseph, who had already given his consent in the marriage to any child from God if it was His will. As husband and wife before the Annunciation, Joseph and Mary were already one. Acting in moral union with Joseph, Mary gave her consent for both of them, not only to the conception of the Child, but also to the salvation of the people of God." *(Dominic De Domenico, O.P., True Devotion to St. Joseph and the Church, #279)*

As the wife of Joseph, Our Lady would not have made this decision without knowing the heart of Joseph. She would have known that, although he might feel intimidated by the reality of being the guardian of the redeemer of all mankind, Joseph loved her and would be faithful to her and Jesus. At the Annunciation, Our Lady didn't express doubt, but wonder in what the angel was telling her. How could this little one from Nazareth be chosen to bear the Messiah?

Joseph wondered the same thing about himself. How could this simple carpenter from Nazareth be a father to the Messiah? Like Mary, he did need an annunciation of his own - the angel's message in his dream - to help him to know that the Father knew he was up to the task of caring for and protecting, both mother and child. Joseph could then give his fiat, his yes, to the Lord and to Our Lady. "In the words of the 'annunciation' by night, Joseph not only heard the divine truth concerning his wife's indescribable vocation; he also heard once again the truth about his own vocation. This 'just' man, who, in the spirit of the noblest traditions of the Chosen People, loved the Virgin of Nazareth and was bound to her by a husband's love, was once again called by God to this love" *(Redemptoris Custos, 19)*.

Although Joseph was not present for Our Lady's annunciation, as her husband, he knew the pull of her Immaculate Heart. He experienced her irresistible beauty and purity. He had no doubt that the Father would have chosen her from all eternity to be the Mother of His Son and that the Son of God would have been drawn in by the perfume of her humility and holiness.

"The nard is a small shrub which exudes a very sweet perfume; it does not rise high like the cedars of Lebanon, but remains in its lowliness, exhaling its perfume with such sweetness that it delights all those who smell it. The holy and most sacred Virgin was this precious nard who never exalted herself on account of anything that was said or done to her; but in her lowliness and littleness, like nard, she gave forth a perfume of such sweet fragrance that it rose to the throne of the Divine Majesty, who was so charmed and delighted by it that He left Heaven to come down here upon earth and become incarnate in the most pure womb of this incomparable Virgin." *(St. Francis de Sales, July 2, 1618 homily)*

Reflection Questions:
Have you experienced moments of wonder and awe in the Lord's will for you? How has He surprised you with a profound gift? Can you imagine increasing the sweetness of these moments by reflecting on them in light of your devotion to Our Lady and Saint Joseph? In one concrete way, how can you give your fiat, your yes, to the Lord today?

_____

_____

_____

_____

_____

_____

_____

\\ WEEK 3 \\ KNOWLEDGE OF THE BLESSED VIRGIN MARY
DAY 18: THE VISITATION

> And Mary said: "My soul proclaims the greatness of the
> Lord; my spirit rejoices in God my savior. For he has
> looked upon his handmaid's lowliness; behold, from now
> on will all ages call me blessed. The Mighty One has done
> great things for me, and holy is his name." *(Luke 1:46-49)*

Some might say that being chosen as the Mother of God might be cause for boasting. I'm not sure anyone would blame someone for a little bit of excitement in the wonder and awe of it all. One could imagine a big celebration could be had to share such news! But what did Our Lady do? She went to *serve* her cousin Elizabeth in her pregnancy. She traveled many miles to celebrate with Elizabeth that the Lord had blessed Zechariah and Elizabeth with a child! She wanted to serve Elizabeth in her labor. Our Lady's desire to serve another, when she was carrying the Messiah is a true testament to her humility. It's also a foreshadowing of the mission of her Son, who, "came to serve and not to be served."

She witnesses to her humility when she proclaims her Magnificat. She proclaims the Lord's greatness, not her own. She rejoices when faced with the fact that she is carrying the Messiah. She remembers her lowliness. She knows she is not worthy of such an honor and that it is a pure gift. She knows that she is blessed to be given the gift of giving flesh to the Son of God. She knows that she has done nothing, but that through her yes, the Lord has done great things and she takes no credit for any of it, but gives all the glory to the holy name of God.

Mary's humility, in giving her fiat and proclaiming her Magnificat, undoes the first human sin. "The sacred Virgin came to regain by her humility what the first Eve had lost by her pride; thus, she reversed Eve's pride and presumption by her humility. When the angel calls her Mother of God, she, plunging herself into the abyss of her nothingness, calls herself His chambermaid; and when

Elizabeth proclaims her blest among women, she replies that his blessing arises from the fact that the Lord had looked upon her lowliness, her littleness..." *(St. Francis de Sales, July 2, 1621)*

When we pray this prayer with Our Lady, we can also pray it with Joseph. When Joseph gives his fiat to the Lord - to love and protect the pregnant Virgin, he makes haste to serve her. The words of his heart, like Elizabeth's might have been, "How does this happen to me that the Mother of my Lord should come to me?" *(Luke 1:43)* He brings her and the child into the home he built for her. In the joy of receiving Our Lady and Jesus into his heart, he can proclaim his Magnificat: "My soul proclaims the greatness of the Lord; my spirit rejoices in God my savior. For he has looked upon his servant's lowliness; behold, from now on will all ages call me blessed. The Mighty One has done great things for me, and holy is his name." Joseph also hastens to serve and not to be served.

Reflection Questions:
When faced with your own struggles, can you have the humility to serve others and be present to them? Can you rejoice in the Lord in the midst of difficulties? How does the humility of Our Lady and Saint Joseph help you to understand and live humility in your life?

_____
_____
_____
_____
_____
_____
_____
_____
_____
_____
_____
_____
_____
_____

\\ Week 3 \\ Knowledge of the Blessed Virgin Mary
Day 19: The Nativity

"And while they were there, the time came for her
to be delivered. And she gave birth to her first-born son
and wrapped him in swaddling clothes, and laid him in a
manger, because there was no place for them in the inn."
(Luke 2:6-7)

Saint Joseph has been given the title of "foster-father" of Jesus. Understandably, there is a need to make sure we don't harbor the belief that Saint Joseph was the biological father of Jesus, but one might see how this title is a slight to Joseph. Adoptive parents honor the biological parents for giving their child life, but the love they have for their children is not "less" than the love the biological parents had when they made the loving choice to gift a couple with the protection and care of their child. In the truest sense of the word, the adoptive parents are the parents of the child. This is true for Saint Joseph, too.

Can you imagine the anxiety in the heart of Joseph when he needs to tell Mary that he's taking her, nine months pregnant, on a donkey to Bethlehem to be enrolled in the census? The worry that must have tempted his heart! Will we be safe? Can I protect her and the Messiah? What if something happens to them? As they set off for Bethlehem, Joseph needed deep faith in the Lord's providence to help him protect mother and child. Mary would have relied on his masculine heart and desire to care for her. Although maybe a little nervous about the journey, she would have trusted her husband. She would have rested in the peace of knowing that Joseph was trustworthy, that he would not allow any harm to come to them.

And then Our Lady's labor began, what then? No room anywhere, but a manger filled with animals. Could the Messiah really be born in a barn, of all places? Am I up to the task of helping my beloved wife birth the Messiah? "Joseph was an eyewitness to this birth, which took place in conditions that, humanly speaking, were embarrassing - a first announcement of that 'self-emptying' *(cf. Phil 2:5-8)* which Christ freely accepted for the forgiveness of sins" *(Saint John Paul II, Redemptoris Custos, 10).*

Joseph received the gift of the Messiah, in a real way, through receiving Him from the Virginal, Immaculate Womb of Mary. In that moment, gazing into the eyes of the Son of God, Joseph welcomed Him into his fatherly heart as his son, his true son, and promised to be the guardian of the mystery "hidden for ages in the mind of God."

"As can be deduced from the gospel texts, Joseph's marriage to Mary is the juridical basis of his fatherhood. It was to assure fatherly protection for Jesus that God chose Joseph to be Mary's spouse. It follows that Joseph's fatherhood - a relationship that places him as close as possible to Christ, to whom every election and predestination is ordered *(cf. Rom 8:28-29)* - comes to pass through marriage to Mary, that is, through the family" *(Saint John Paul II, Redemptoris Custos, 7).*

Reflection Questions:
Do you ever feel like you are not up to the task that the Lord is asking of you? In those moments, do you rely on the grace of the Lord or do you fall into self-reliance? Is your heart open to receive others as spiritual sons and daughters? To love them, as if they are your own, to guide and protect them? Ask Saint Joseph today about how his heart received Jesus into his heart and ask for the grace to receive Jesus in yours.

\\ Week 3 \\ Knowledge of the Blessed Virgin Mary
Day 20: The Assumption

"But the Virgin, coming up to Heaven into the court of her Son, brought with her so much gold of charity, so many perfumes of devotion and virtue, such a great quantity of precious stones of patience and sufferings that she had borne in His Name, that reducing them all to merits we can truly say that never was so great a quantity brought to Heaven. Never did anyone present so much to her Son as did this holy Lady." *(Saint Francis de Sales, Homily – August 15, 1602)*

The ache and longing each of us feels for union and communion is the ache and longing for heaven. We long to be united with God for all eternity. "Heaven is the ultimate end and fulfillment of the deepest human longings, the state of supreme, definitive happiness" *(Catechism of the Catholic Church, 1024)*. We long to find every desire fulfilled and see God face to face in a rapture that will never end. Because of our pull toward sin (concupiscence), we are tempted to aim that desire for fulfillment toward other people and things, but nothing will fully satisfy us like heaven.

Our Lady understood and lived that ache and longing for heaven like no one else on earth. She had been united with the Holy Trinity in a uniquely beautiful and fulfilling way. Because of her Immaculate Conception, free from original sin, Our Lady experienced union and communion with God, and especially with her son, Jesus in a most powerful way. As she experienced the Passion, death, and Resurrection of her son, her mother's heart was left on earth to experience a deep ache and longing for union and communion with Him.

The Church professes its belief that Our Lady, free of original sin, was Assumed body and soul into heaven at the time of her death. This Assumption was the fulfillment of her ache and longing for union and communion with her son and the Holy Trinity. One could imagine that her ache and longing for union and communion also connected with her desire to be reunited with Saint Joseph. We experience this ache and longing in the death of our loved ones. We feel that chasm between heaven and earth in the depth of our hearts. We long to be united with our loved ones again and our faith can give us the confident hope that this longing will be fulfilled when we will all, the communion of saints, be united with God and each other for all eternity. Jesus and Mary knew this longing and this hope in the death of Saint Joseph. Although Scripture does not mention the death of Saint Joseph, he ceases to be mentioned in Scripture beyond the Finding of the Child Jesus in the Temple, we can assume that he was no longer present at the time of the beginning of Jesus' public ministry.

Could Saint Joseph have been given the gift of assumption into heaven, as well? Although not a defined dogma of the Church, some theologians base belief on Saint Joseph's assumption on this passage from the Gospel of Matthew. "Many bodies of the saints who had fallen asleep arose; and coming forth out of the tombs after His resurrection, they came into the holy city and appeared to many" *(Mt 27:52-53)*. Even Pope John XXIII, in his homily on the feast of the Ascension of Our Lord on May 26, 1960, made the statement that the Assumption of Saint Joseph "is worthy of pious belief."

One could imagine that Jesus would have desired the union and communion with Our Lady and Saint Joseph in heaven. No two people lived devotion, virtue, patience, and suffering like Our Lady and Saint Joseph. No two people knew the heart of Jesus like Mary and Joseph. One can only imagine the joy at that reunion if Joseph was also assumed into Heaven! The fulfillment of the ache for communion was Our Lady's Assumption, as Jesus and Saint Joseph welcomed her home, body and soul.

Reflection Questions:
How do you attempt to satisfy the ache and longing of your heart with anything other than God or the hope for heaven? If you have lost loved ones, can you give them over to the care of the Holy Family and have confident hope in your communion with them again in heaven?

\\ WEEK 3 \\ KNOWLEDGE OF THE BLESSED VIRGIN MARY
DAY 21: RELATIONSHIP WITH THE TRINITY

"O my God, Trinity whom I adore, help me to become utterly forgetful of myself so that I may establish myself in you, as changeless and calm as though my soul were already in eternity. Let nothing disturb my peace nor draw me forth from you, O my unchanging God, at every moment may I penetrate more deeply into the depths of your mystery.

Give peace to my soul; make it your heaven, your cherished dwelling-place and the place of your repose. Let me never leave you there alone, but keep me there, wholly attentive, wholly alert in my faith, wholly adoring and fully given up to your creative action."
St. Elizabeth of the Trinity

Our Lady experienced the most unique relationship with the Holy Trinity. If we reflect on each unique relationship, we will be encouraged to encounter the three Persons of the Trinity in our own lives.

The Father, from all eternity, desired Our Lady to be the Mother of the Son of God. He did so by entering into the marital embrace of Our Lady's parents, Saints Joachim and Anne, to create Our Lady without original sin. The Immaculate Conception was the beginning of the Father's plan to create within Our Lady, a womb immaculate and worthy to receive the Son of God. "The Father bending down to this beautiful creature, who was so unaware of her own beauty, willed that she be the Mother in time of Him whose Father He is in eternity" *(Saint Elizabeth of the Trinity, Heaven in Faith, 39).*

The Holy Spirit overshadowed Our Lady at the Annunciation when Our Lady gave her fiat, her yes to become the Mother of God. Our Lady opened her heart and her body to the Holy Spirit to participate in the creation of the child Jesus. "In Mary, the Holy Spirit fulfills the plan of the Father's loving goodness. Through the Holy Spirit, the Virgin conceives and gives birth to the Son of God. By the Holy Spirit's power and her faith, her virginity became uniquely fruitful." *(Catechism of the Catholic Church, 723)*

The Son was conceived within the womb of Our Lady. She provided the Son of God with a pure ark in which to receive nourishment and protection. For nine months, the Son of God grew within her womb. She knew the Son, her son, most intimately. She felt him kick inside of her. She gave birth to him and nursed Him at her breast. Her yes gave life to the Son of God. "In fact, the One whom she conceived as man by the Holy Spirit, who truly became her Son according to the flesh, was none other than the Father›s eternal Son, the second person of the Holy Trinity. Hence the Church confesses that Mary is truly 'Mother of God' (Theotokos)" *(Catechism of the Catholic Church, 495).*

As unique as Our Lady's relationship with each Person of the Trinity was, Saint Joseph models a unique relationship as well. The Father chose Joseph to be the husband of Our Lady and the father of Jesus. He sent an angel to him to encourage him not to be afraid. The angel confirmed for Joseph that the child was conceived through the power of the Holy Spirit. Throughout his life, Joseph had a uniquely intimate relationship with the Son. He protected, cared for, and guided Him. He spent each day of his life teaching Him the things of the world and the miraculous gift He was to the Holy Family.

The unity of the Holy Family points us clearly to the unity of the Holy Trinity. We, too, are called to have an intimate relationship with the Holy Trinity. Mary and Joseph's openness and unique relationship with each of the Persons of the Holy Trinity are models for us of the importance of uniquely encountering each of them in our own lives.

Reflection Questions:
How do you encounter each Person of the Trinity in your prayer life? Is there one, or more, Person of the Trinity that you know you

need to grow in intimacy with through your prayer life? Ask Our Lady and Saint Joseph to help you to grow in your relationship with the Holy Trinity.

_____
_____
_____
_____
_____
_____
_____
_____
_____
_____
_____
_____
_____
_____
_____
_____
_____
_____
_____
_____
_____
_____
_____
_____
_____
_____
_____
_____
_____
_____
_____
_____
_____
_____
_____

WEEK 3 PRAYERS

Litany of the Blessed Virgin
Lord, *have mercy on us.*
Christ, *have mercy on us.*
Lord, *have mercy on us.*

Father all-powerful, *have mercy on us.*
Jesus, Eternal Son of the Father, Redeemer of the world, *save us.*
Spirit of the Father and the Son, boundless life of both,
sanctify us.
Holy Trinity, *hear us.*

Holy Mary,	*pray for us.* (after each line)
Holy Mother of God,	*pray for us.*
Holy Virgin of virgins,	...
Mother of Christ,	...
Mother of divine grace,	
Mother most pure,	
Mother most chaste,	
Mother inviolate,	
Mother undefiled,	
Mother most amiable,	
Mother most admirable,	
Mother of good counsel,	
Mother of our Creator,	
Mother of our Savior,	
Virgin most prudent,	
Virgin most venerable,	
Virgin most renowned,	
Virgin most powerful,	
Virgin most merciful,	
Virgin most faithful,	
Mirror of justice,	
Seat of wisdom,	
Cause of our joy,	
Spiritual vessel,	
Vessel of honor,	

Singular vessel of devotion,
Mystical rose,
Tower of David,
Tower of ivory,
House of gold,
Ark of the covenant,
Gate of Heaven,
Morning star,
Health of the sick,
Refuge of sinners,
Comforter of the afflicted,
Help of Christians,
Queen of angels,
Queen of patriarchs,
Queen of prophets,
Queen of apostles,
Queen of martyrs,
Queen of confessors,
Queen of virgins,
Queen of all saints,
Queen conceived without original sin,
Queen assumed into heaven,
Queen of the most holy Rosary,
Queen of peace.

Lamb of God, who takes away the sins of the world,
Spare us, O Lord.
Lamb of God, who takes away the sins of the world,
Graciously hear us O Lord.
Lamb of God, who takes away the sins of the world,
Have mercy on us.

Pray for us, O holy Mother of God.
That we may be made worthy of the promises of Christ.

Let us pray:
Grant, O Lord God, we beseech You, that we Your servants may rejoice in continual health of mind and body; and, through the glorious intercession of Blessed Mary ever Virgin, may be freed

from present sorrow, and enjoy eternal gladness. Through Christ our Lord. Amen.

Second Prayer to St. Joseph
We turn to you, blessed Joseph, in our affliction, and having implored the help of your holy Spouse, we now, with hearts filled with confidence, earnestly beg you also to take us under your protection. By that charity which you were united to the Immaculate Virgin Mother of God, and by that fatherly love with which cherished the Child Jesus, we beseech you and we humbly pray that you will look down with gracious eyes upon that inheritance which Jesus Christ purchased by His blood, and will provide for us in our need by your power and strength.

Defend, O most watchful guardian of the Holy Family, the chosen off-spring of Jesus Christ. Keep from us, O most loving Father, all deceit of error and corruption. Aid us from on high, most valiant defender, in this conflict with the powers of darkness. And even as you rescued the Child Jesus from the peril of His life, so now defend God's Holy Church from the snares of the enemy and from all adversity. Shield us ever under your patronage, that, following your example and strengthened by your help, we may live a holy life, die a happy death, and attain to everlasting joy in Heaven. Amen.

\\ WEEK 4 \\ KNOWLEDGE OF SAINT JOSEPH
DAY 22: DEVOTION TO SAINT JOSEPH

"We judge it of deep utility for the Christian people, continually to invoke with great piety and trust, together with the Virgin-Mother of God, her chaste Spouse, the Blessed Joseph; and We regard it as most certain that this will be most pleasing to the Virgin herself." (*Quamquam Pluries, Encyclical on St. Joseph by Pope Leo XIII*)

"While it is important for the Church to profess the virginal conception of Jesus, it is no less important to uphold Mary's marriage to Joseph, because juridically Joseph's fatherhood depends on it. Thus, one understands why the generations are listed according to the genealogy of Joseph: "Why," St. Augustine asks, "should they not be according to Joseph? Was he not Mary's husband?... Scripture states, through the authority of an angel, that he was her husband. Do not fear, says the angel, to take Mary your wife, for that which is conceived in her is of the Holy Spirit. Joseph was told to name the child, although not born from his seed. She will bear a son, the angel says, and you will call him Jesus. Scripture recognizes that Jesus is not born of Joseph's seed, since in his concern about the origin of Mary's pregnancy, Joseph is told that it is of the Holy Spirit. Nonetheless, he is not deprived of his fatherly authority from the moment that he is told to name the child. Finally, even the Virgin Mary, well aware that she has not conceived Christ as a result of conjugal relations with Joseph, still calls him Christ's father."

The Son of Mary is also Joseph's Son by virtue of the marriage bond that unites them: "By reason of their faithful marriage both of them deserve to be called Christ's parents, not only his mother, but also his father, who was a parent in the same way that he was the mother's spouse: in mind, not in the flesh." (*Redemptoris Custos, 7*)

———

In this last line especially, we find the radical need for a devotion to Saint Joseph. We understand the value of devotion to Mary because she is the mother of God. We understand that as a physical reality- her womb bore the person of Jesus Christ. Joseph is also the father of God! Why would we not say this is so? Because we, in our culture, all too easily separate the mind from the body. If Joseph is the father of Jesus "in mind, not in the flesh," is he any less a father? No. He is every bit as much a father as Mary is a mother, because we understand the integrity of the human person as spirit and flesh. We always maintain the awesome mystery of the Incarnation, and never seek to reduce it to something our minds can fully grasp. But one thing we can say, because we believe in the unity of the spirit and body in the human person, is that a father in mind is a father in fact.

Joseph, therefore, is a true father of Jesus, God Incarnate, as Mary is a true mother. We owe devotion to Mary, the mother of God, because she was chosen from the beginning to conceive Jesus, and we owe devotion to Joseph, the father of God, because he was chosen from the beginning to father Jesus.

Our society and our church are in dire need of Saint Joseph - but why? What has our society come to believe about the human person? About the family? About the role of men and women? About marriage and the role of husbands and wives? Our world is suffering from a severe misunderstanding of all these things.

How have you suffered from these misunderstandings? It is easy to think of things in "us vs. them" terms. "The world" is lost but we have the truth. That may be true when it comes to our faith, but what about the deeply ingrained "sense of self" that we inherit from the world.

Do you ever think of yourself as a "spirit trapped in a body"? Do you think of Heaven as a place your spirit goes once it sheds and leaves behind these dirty bodies?

These heresies of disintegration lead to other false ideas. We misunderstand the nature of sexual complementarity. How

83

many of us believe that gender differences simply need to be "endured"? "Men are from Mars, Women are from Venus" has become a deeply ingrained paradigm that most of us assume to be true. While the differences are real, this mindset lacks any sense of the **collaboration and unity** we are called to develop in our relationships. We miss the true meaning of marriage.

The most important fruit of marriage is holiness, which is another way of saying that marriage is a vocation ordered towards bringing Jesus into this world through your union with him. This happens not just in the marriage of Mary and Joseph, but through the marriage of every man and woman.

We need to submit our vocations - whether it is marriage or something else - to the perfect model for every vocation found in the marriage of Joseph and Mary. Their model of perfect self-gift, perfect complementarity, perfect collaboration, and perfect unity will correct us out of whatever errors we harbor and open us up to truly bringing Jesus into this world through us.

"At the culmination of the history of salvation, when God reveals his love for humanity through the gift of the Word, it is precisely the marriage of Mary and Joseph that brings to realization in full "freedom" the "spousal gift of self" in receiving and expressing such a love." In this great undertaking which is the renewal of all things in Christ, marriage-it too purified and renewed-becomes a new reality, a sacrament of the New Covenant. We see that at the beginning of the New Testament, as at the beginning of the Old, there is a married couple. But whereas Adam and Eve were the source of evil which was unleashed on the world, Joseph and Mary are the summit from which holiness spreads all over the earth. The Savior began the work of salvation by this virginal and holy union, wherein is manifested his all-powerful will to purify and sanctify the family - that sanctuary of love and cradle of life." (*Redemptoris Custos, 7*)

Let us welcome Joseph, then, into our devotional paradigm of the path to holiness. Jesus came to us through Mary and Joseph, and so we can go to Jesus through Mary and Joseph. They are our parents in the faith as they are the parents of Christ whom we seek.

Reflection Questions:
Do you harbor some deep unconscious belief about Jesus that he must have been like an angel living on earth? What basic, normal, seemingly mundane and even boring parts of your life could you connect to the life of Jesus, Mary, and Joseph to realize the true divine potential he invites you to?

Every single one of us longs for the father's gaze. We want to be seen and chosen by our dads. It is biological, psychological, and spiritual. We are predisposed for this longing from the moment of our conception and enter into the world with this longing that never ceases. Mom's gaze comes easier, we expect it, and it is our primary necessity to remain secure in our being as we are. It is the gaze of the father, however, which draws us out of ourselves to become more.

When children have the gaze of the father, they look to the father with trust and security, and then to God. Fathers are called to be the link between heaven and earth. Fathers are an icon of God the father to their children.

Jesus in his humanity was no exception to this need, and he had the gaze of Saint Joseph, who had a, "share in the corresponding love that has its origin in the Father "from whom every family in heaven and on earth is named" *(Eph 3:15).* Joseph showed Jesus "by a special gift from heaven, all the natural love, all the affectionate solicitude that a father's heart can know." (*Redemptoris Custos*, 8)

Saint Joseph gazes upon each one of us with this same paternal love. He gazes upon each one of us called to union with Christ as we become adopted sons, not only of the Father in Heaven who formed Heaven and Earth, but of the father from earth, now in Heaven, who formed Jesus's human personality.

Joseph can rightfully be called "father of all the faithful." This is a title that reminds us of Abraham, the first father in faith. Abraham's patriarchy is established because of his faith. Recall that Abraham's faith was most exemplified by his willingness to sacrifice his son Isaac, even though God told him he would be the father of a multitude of descendants. He stood there, looking at his (only) son, knowing God promised him many generations, yet also hearing God ask him to give his son up for sacrifice.

Joseph, also, was promised to be the father of many descendants in the faith. He knew Jesus was conceived of the Holy Spirit, he knew the prophecies, the foreshadowing, and the typology (which is a fancy word for all the ways the Old Testament foreshadowed everything that was happening in their little home). Yet, as we reflected on earlier, he also heard Simeon's prophecy. He knew it would not be easy. As soon as Jesus was born Joseph was facing life-threatening circumstances. As he watched Jesus grow and taught him how to be a man, he knew there was immense pain in the future for his beloved family. He accepted all this with deep trust when he said yes. Joseph is the perfect father. He loves us first with a fully committed, present, and affirming gaze. It is this father's gaze, which says, "I see you, you've got what it takes, you're created for greatness." Then he leads by example. He shows us how to have faith in the face of all difficulties, even if it means personal sacrifice. He enables us for greatness, and he shows us how to live it out.

Reflection Questions:
How might you need the father's gaze in your life? Do you feel empowered by the love of one who has gone before you to follow the path and achieve greatness in your life? Do you feel secure in the embrace of being loved by a powerful and strong love? How will developing a deeper relationship with Joseph as father help you to become a better version of yourself?

Much has been written on the silence of Saint Joseph. It's one quality of Saint Joseph we can easily jump to without having to interpret or assume too much. There's simply nothing recorded of anything Joseph ever said in Scripture. Without realizing it, many people can disregard the silence of Joseph as a quaint way of explaining away the absence of Scripture accounting for anything he ever said. This is unfortunate, because there is so much that Saint Joseph can teach us about silence as a father guiding his children.

Mary and Joseph both had the deepest interior lives possible, living in the presence of the Word Made Flesh. As Cardinal Sarah says in *The Power of Silence*, "Silence is not an exile of speech. It is the love of the one Word. Conversely, the abundance of words is the symptom of doubt. Incredulity is always talkative." Joseph dwelt continually in the presence of the Word, saw him face to face and loved him with a father's love. What greater love is there than that of a mother and father? If silence is the love of the one Word, there was no greater silence than that of the actual mother and father of the Word.

Cardinal Sarah continues: "We often forget that Christ loved to be silent. He set out for the desert, not to go into exile, but to encounter God. And at the most crucial moment of his life, when there was screaming on all sides, covering him with all sorts of lies and calumnies, when the high priest asked him, 'Have you no answer to make?' Jesus preferred silence" *(Sarah, p.80)*.

"Catholics no longer know that silence is sacred because it is God's dwelling place. How can we rediscover the sense of silence as the manifestation of God? This is the tragedy of the modern world: man separates himself from God because he no longer believes in the value of silence" *(Sarah, p. 80)*.

Saint Joseph can help us rediscover the manifestation of God in his silence. "The Gospels speak exclusively of what Joseph 'did.' Still, they allow us to discover in his 'actions' - shrouded in silence as they are - an aura of deep contemplation. Joseph was in daily contact with the mystery 'hidden from ages past,' and which 'dwelt' under his roof. This explains, for example, why Saint Teresa of Jesus, the great reformer of the Carmelites, promoted the renewal of veneration to Saint Joseph in Western Christianity" (*Redemptoris Custos*, 25).

Part of the message of Our Lady of America is a call to deeper devotion to Saint Joseph as well. One suggestion to facilitate this devotion is an observance of First Wednesdays dedicated to Saint Joseph. To participate in this devotion, one must pray the rosary while meditating on the mysteries in light of Saint Joseph's perspective, and receive Holy Communion uniting oneself to the heart of Joseph and receiving Jesus as Joseph received him in the Nativity. This is a beautiful practice whenever one receives Jesus. What greater interior recollection can you imagine than the sense of awe-inspiring mystery and cosmically reverberating silence experienced in the hearts of Joseph and Mary as the Word Incarnate passed from the womb of Mary into Joseph's arms?

Reflection Questions:
What is keeping you from interior silence in your life? If Cardinal Sarah is right, the lack of silence corresponds to a lack of faith. Are there ways your mind stays noisy because there are things you don't trust God to take care of? If you follow the thought-trails that are loudest, you will most likely find attachments God is inviting you to surrender to Him.

\\ WEEK 4 \\ KNOWLEDGE OF SAINT JOSEPH
DAY 25: INTERIOR RECOLLECTION AND DISCERNMENT

Continuing from our theme yesterday, we look again to the silence taught by the recollection of Saint Joseph. He taught Jesus the silence with which he encountered God, and the silence with which he discerned the action God willed for him in any given moment. As Thomas Merton said, "The silence of God should teach us when to speak and when not to speak" *(Thoughts in Solitude, 42)*

We must develop a deep interior life, which means a heart and mind tuned into the presence of God. God is not found in the noise of life but in the silence. When we allow that silence to envelope our inner world, we position ourselves before God so that He may speak to us.

Saint Mother Teresa wrote in *In the Heart of the World*, "We need to find God, and he cannot be found in noises and restlessness. God is the friend of silence... The more we receive in silent prayer, the more we can give in active life. We need silence to be able to touch souls. The essential thing is not what we say, but what God says to us and through us."

What is our noise and restlessness? It is our lack of trust. We act as if we can avoid suffering for ourselves or others by ruminating on our problems. We allow the noise of our thoughts to drown out the silence of God. We also let the noise of our distractions keep us from the presence of God. We are afraid of what we will find in the silence, as we are reflected back to ourselves in God's presence, and so we avoid it all cost with whatever temporary gratification of attention floats by.

Discernment is the process by which the noise of our broken and imperfect selves quiets down - dies even - so that all that remains is the silence in which we can commune with God. There, His thoughts and our thoughts line up. His desire and our desires line up. We can experience the deepest movements of our hearts in this state and realize that it is His heart moving in us. This is the heart of discernment.

"The total sacrifice, whereby Joseph surrendered his whole existence to the demands of the Messiah's coming into his home, becomes understandable only in the light of his profound interior life. It was from this interior life that 'very singular commands and consolations came, bringing him also the logic and strength that belong to simple and clear souls, and giving him the power of making great decisions-such as the decision to put his liberty immediately at the disposition of the divine designs, to make over to them also his legitimate human calling, his conjugal happiness, to accept the conditions, the responsibility and the burden of a family, but, through an incomparable virginal love, to renounce that natural conjugal love that is the foundation and nourishment of the family." (*Redemptoris Custos*, 25)

This was the necessary condition of Joseph (and Mary's) life so that they could make the radical decisions that brought God into the world, provided for and protected him, and joined him in his salvific mission. God gives each one of us the capacity to live with this radical acceptance of His will, and the means by which to know it through interior recollection. It is a knowing that can only occur when we do our part to create the stillness inside of us, to draw deeper into interior recollection with the trustful surrender to the goodness of God, and to wait upon him to stir our hearts to action.

Reflection Questions:
What is at the root of your distractions when you attempt to recollect yourself in silence? What are you afraid of? What is holding you back?

_____

_____

_____

_____

_____

_____

Today we continue to reap the harvest that comes from Joseph's lessons on interior silence and recollection. Silence first brings us into the encounter with God, it opens us then to the Holy Spirit and the Word He speaks into our hearts, and finally it forms the foundation from which we learn true charity.

"In Joseph, the apparent tension between the active and the contemplative life finds an ideal harmony that is only possible for those who possess the perfection of charity. Following Saint Augustine's well-known distinction between the love of the truth (caritas veritatis) and the practical demands of love (necessitas caritatis), we can say that Joseph experienced both love of the truth - that pure contemplative love of the divine Truth which radiated from the humanity of Christ - and the demands of love - that equally pure and selfless love required for his vocation to safeguard and develop the humanity of Jesus, which was inseparably linked to his divinity" *(Redemptoris Custos, 27)*.

The contemplative life is typically considered to be the life of dwelling constantly in the presence of Truth and Love, while the active life is typically considered one of outward love, manifesting the love of God in the world towards others. Sometimes the active life can also be conflated with busyness. We are used to the "Martha/Mary" distinction, which comes from Jesus reproving Martha for being busy while Mary simply sits in the presence of Jesus undisturbed. Saint John Paul II points us to the ideal harmony we are created for found in Joseph, one of bringing together interior recollection focused in the Divine Indwelling and the exterior actions of love that flow seamlessly from the integrated life we are made for.

Our actions, from the movements of our minds and hearts we choose to sit with, entertain, or nurture, to the outward expression of words and behaviors towards ourselves and others, are all meant to flow from this contemplative recollection in the presence of God. We receive God's presence and love, and it flows through us in one seamless movement. This is how our communion with God expands outwards to our communion with each other.

This communion is most often manifest outwardly in communication. Communication is the art of receiving from others and then making ourselves vulnerable in the gift of self in return. The less silent we are - the less recollected - the less practiced we are at receiving. This lack of experience in receiving makes it extremely difficult to truly listen to others. We suffer tremendously in our culture of noise and distraction, which ultimately makes us all neophytes at communication.

Cardinal Sarah once again clarifies this for us: "In order to listen, it is necessary to keep quiet. I do not mean merely a sort of constraint to be physically silent and not to interrupt what someone else is saying, but rather an interior silence, in other words, a silence that not only is directed toward receiving the other person's words but also reflects a heart overflowing with a humble love, capable of full attention, friendly and welcome and voluntary self-denial, and strong with the awareness of our poverty... The silence of listening is a form of attention, a gift of self to the other, and a mark of moral generosity. It should manifest an awareness of our humility so as to agree to receive from another person a gift that God is giving us. For the other person is always a treasure and a precious gift that God offers to help us grow in humility, humanity, and nobility" (*The Power of Silence*, 81).

The gift of a receptive and listening heart and mind is one of the greatest gifts we can give someone.

This gets more difficult if the content of conversation challenges our own points of view. We need Joseph's help here. He models for us the perfect stance to take in these situations. We can trust God above all things like he did, surrendering ourselves to Him and believing that no matter what, all will be well. Then we can let our hearts and minds be quiet, resting in His presence. This recollection teaches us how to be open and silent then in the presence of others - even if they are "wrong" - because we know there is a bigger picture. We can be receptive first and foremost of the gift this person is in his or her being. We can be receptive then of the dignity of his or her own experience and the thoughts and feelings it leads to - again, even if it is misdirected or needs to be refined. With this open receptivity and listening heart we will offer an experience of encounter to the other. We will encounter the other. Encounter itself heals many wounds.

This takes practice and time to develop. We are capable of this recollection though, and the possibility for receptive listening that flows from it. We are students in the School of Love, Saint Joseph is our teacher. If we study and do our homework, we can learn the lesson.

Reflection Questions:
What specific issues are most difficult for you to communicate effectively about with others? Looking through today's lens, what issues of trust might be underlying your difficulty in listening in these conversations? What ruminations do you find yourself distracted by in these areas? How can Joseph's model of trust help you connect to a better way of handling these situations?

A further virtue of Saint Joseph that he leads us to and models for us is humility. This is a difficult virtue for many to understand. It is an even more difficult virtue to attain. One of the most difficult aspects of it is the self-reflective nature of pride. As soon as one thinks he has humility, he loses it. How are we to understand this virtue?

The words of the Papal Preacher, a Franciscan by the name of Father Raniero Cantalamessa, helps us understand more deeply the virtue of humility. He says, "Humility, per se, in the most perfect degree, is not in being little, it is not in feeling that oneself is little or proclaiming oneself little. It is in making oneself little, and not out of some necessity or personal utility, but out of love, to 'raise' others. Thus was Jesus' humility; He made himself so little, in fact, to the point of "annulling" himself for us" *(Second Advent Homily, 2013).*

Humility is not littleness or even the feeling of littleness because these things can be attributed to pathology. There can be "false humility" that leads to the same kinds of feelings. Humility, in Cantalemessa's terms, is related to service. This is the service that Jesus models for us and calls us to in the Gospel. "The Son of man came to be served and not to serve" *(Mt 20:28).* Jesus tells us that if we wish to be first, we must be last. He explains that this means we are meant to be the servant of all.

This, of course, is the service that Joseph modeled for Jesus and all of us. He put his life totally at the service of God's will. He was called to serve God by devoting himself to Mary in a virginal marriage, completely dedicated to her and the child they would bring into the world together, while at the same time totally sacrificing the marital joys of physical love.

Joseph knew he was raising the Messiah; yet how much humility it must have taken to carry out this mission on a daily basis! We don't know how old Jesus was when Joseph passed, but we can only imagine what it was like living out of the simplicity of normal and basic family life raising the Son of God! Joseph and Mary's neighbors had no idea who they were raising! Their friends and family looked on and saw nothing remarkable- this was the testament to the simplicity with which Joseph and Mary must have carried themselves in literally the most important mission that has ever been given to any human person in the history of all time.

Joseph was called to raise the Messiah, the Son of God. He was called to teach him how to walk, talk, work and pray. He was called to teach Jesus how to love in the context of simple family life. That was it. He was not called to reveal Christ's mission, he was not called to raise the dead, or cast out demons. He was also called to be married to the most beautiful and holy woman that's ever walked the face of the earth, love her with the most undying and passionate love that any man has ever felt for any woman, and do it all while maintaining perfectly pure and chaste celibacy.

This kind of service necessitates sacrifices that only Joseph in the secret depths of his own heart could ever know. This is not a public martyrdom with widespread accolades, but one that didn't register with anyone else around him. This is the littleness and servitude of humility that leaves nothing for pride to grow fat on. This is the humility we can all learn how to grow in.

Reflection Questions:
What are you called to do in service and love that you balk at because you won't receive "credit?" What hidden sacrifices could you make more consistently but don't? How are you called to grow in humility by making yourself "last" without counting the cost?

_____

_____

_____

_____

_____

_____

Our reflections on Saint Joseph culminate today in what may be his finest characteristic, and the one with which he is most well-known. Purity. Often the Holy Family is invoked as the *Sacred Heart of Jesus*, the *Immaculate Heart of Mary*, and the *Pure Heart of Joseph*.

Joseph began the same as all of us in concupiscence, yet he represents the fullness of what we are all called to. This is the great hope we receive from the life and example of Saint Joseph.

By his sacrifice united to the sacrifice of Mary, eternal divinity entered into time and space. The virginal marriage of Mary and Joseph provided the foundation and context for the marriage of heaven and earth. Joseph, who began with the same wound of Adam as all of us, surrendered himself to the will of God so thoroughly in overcoming his concupiscence, living in passionate and total devotion to his wife, and virginally loving her with so great a love as to provide appropriate passage for the Holy Spirit Himself to incarnate, generate, and mature within the context of their marriage.

"The marriage of Mary with Joseph conceals within itself, at the same time, the mystery of the perfect communion of persons, of Man and Woman in the conjugal covenant and at the same time the mystery of this singular 'continence for the kingdom of heaven': a continence that served the most perfect 'fruitfulness of the Holy Spirit' in the history of salvation. Indeed, it was in some way the absolute fullness of that spiritual fruitfulness, because precisely in Mary and Joseph's covenant in marriage and continence, the gift of the Incarnation of the Eternal Word was realized" (*Theology of the Body, 75:3*).

Saint John Paul II also taught that celibate men and women must in some way realize the human vocation to fatherhood and motherhood, in a spiritual sense, as they truly foster the fertility of a life lived radically for God, receptive to the Holy Spirit, and generating "new life" in Jesus through their prayers and intercession of their lives.

At the same time, married men and women are called to make gifts of themselves, to sacrifice themselves for the good of the other, to follow Christ by "taking up his Cross and following Him." In this way they are meant to live with some share in the self-surrender that is embraced by celibate men and women. The two vocations, celibacy and marriage, are meant to be "co-educative." Married couples and celibate individuals teach each other some aspect of the life we are all called to live. Married couples can show celibate people what it actually looks like to surrender to another person on a day-to-day basis, and what the fruit (babies) of that total gift of self can really look like. Celibate men and women show to married couples what it looks like to remain devoted to God in all things, with eyes towards our final destiny which is Heaven - total union with God - without counting the cost of surrender or valuing too highly things that are passing. God has willed for both to co-exist, one does not exist without the other!

"Christian celibacy 'must lead in its normal development to 'fatherhood' or 'motherhood' in the spiritual sense... in a way analogous to conjugal love. On its part, physical generation also fully corresponds to its meaning only if it is completed by fatherhood and motherhood in the spirit, whose expression and fruit is the whole educational work of the parents in regard to the children born of their union" (*Theology of the Body, 78:5*).

In Mary and Joseph we find both. In their marriage we encounter a deep mystery. We find contained within their family the lesson of total self-surrender and giftedness to the other, and the fruitfulness that is so profound as to be the Incarnation itself. Our self-surrender is meant to bear the fruit of Jesus taking over in our hearts, so that we "decrease so that he may increase," while their self-surrender was meant to bear the fruit of Jesus Himself entering our world in history. What hope! What joy! What mission we find in their example! They show us what is possible, in the normal context of basic human life! What can be more important than this? We are not all asked to sacrifice what they were asked to sacrifice, but we are all asked to say yes to sacrificing totally whatever God wills. It is this total abandonment and surrender of selves that unites our lives to God so thoroughly that he becomes present in us and through us in the world.

Saint Joseph, Pure of Heart, help us be pure like you. Help us surrender ourselves to God so thoroughly that Jesus is born in us. Help us hold nothing back. Whatever selfish desires hold us back - help us let them go. Whatever fears hold us back - help us let them go. Whatever doubts hold us back - help us let them go.

Reflection Questions:
What is your heart holding onto that is not of God? What do you need Joseph's help most to let go of?

_____
_____
_____
_____
_____
_____
_____
_____
_____
_____
_____
_____
_____
_____
_____
_____
_____
_____
_____
_____
_____
_____

WEEK 4 PRAYERS

Litany of Saint Joseph
Lord, *have mercy on us.*
Christ, *have mercy on us.*
Lord, *have mercy on us.*

Father all-powerful, *have mercy on us.*
Jesus, Eternal Son of the Father, Redeemer of the world, *save us.*
Spirit of the Father and the Son, boundless life of both,
sanctify us.
Holy Trinity, *hear us.*

Holy Mary,	*pray for us.* (after each line)
Saint Joseph,	*pray for us.*
Renowned offspring of David,	...
Light of Patriarchs,	...

Spouse of the Mother of God,
Chaste guardian of the Virgin,
Foster-father of the Son of God,
Diligent protector of Christ,
Head of the Holy Family,
Joseph most just,
Joseph most chaste,
Joseph most prudent,
Joseph most strong,
Joseph most obedient,
Joseph most faithful,
Mirror of patience,
Lover of poverty,
Model of artisans,
Glory of home life,
Guardian of virgins,
Pillar of families,
Solace of the wretched,
Hope of the sick,
Patron of the dying,

106

Terror of demons,
Protector of Holy Church,

Lamb of God, who take away the sins of the world,
Spare us, O Lord.
Lamb of God, who take away the sins of the world,
Graciously hear us, O Lord.
Lamb of God, who take away the sins of the world,
Have mercy on us.

He made him the lord of His house:
And ruler of all His substance.

Let us pray.
O God, who in your unspeakable providence chose blessed
Joseph to be the spouse of your own most holy Mother: grant, we
beseech you, that we may deserve to have him for our intercessor
in heaven, whom we reverence as our defender on earth: who
lives and reigns world without end. Amen.

Litany of Humility
O Jesus! Meek and humble of heart, hear me.
From the desire of being esteemed, deliver me Jesus
From the desire of being loved, deliver me Jesus
From the desire of being extolled, deliver me Jesus
From the desire of being honored, deliver me Jesus
From the desire of being praised, deliver me Jesus
From the desire of being preferred, deliver me Jesus
From the desire of being consulted, deliver me Jesus
From the desire of being approved, deliver me Jesus.
From the fear of being humiliated, deliver me Jesus
From the fear of being despised, deliver me Jesus
From the fear of suffering rebukes, deliver me Jesus
From the fear of being calumniated, deliver me Jesus
From the fear of being forgotten, deliver me Jesus
From the fear of being ridiculed, deliver me Jesus
From the fear of being wronged, deliver me Jesus
From the fear of being suspected, deliver me Jesus

That others may be loved more than I, Jesus, grant me the grace to desire it.

That others may be esteemed more than I, Jesus, grant me the grace to desire it

That in the opinion of the world, others may increase and I may decrease, Jesus, grant me the grace to desire it.

That others may be chosen and I set aside, Jesus, grant me the grace to desire it.

That others may be praised and I unnoticed, Jesus, grant me the grace to desire it.

That others may be preferred to me in everything, Jesus, grant me the grace to desire it.

That others become holier than I, provided that I may become as holy as I should, Jesus, grant me the grace to desire it.

Amen.

\\ WEEK 5 \\ KNOWLEDGE OF JESUS CHRIST
DAY 29: INCARNATION

"Christ Jesus, who, though he was in the form of God, did not count equality with God a thing to be grasped, but emptied himself, taking the form of a servant, being born in the likeness of men. And being found in human form he humbled himself and became obedient unto death, even death on a cross." *(Ph 2:5-8).*

The reality of the Incarnation is one of the greatest mysteries of the Christian faith. If we don't stammer and stutter in its recitation, stumbling over ways to think about it, understand it, or explain it, we are probably not probing the mystery deeply enough.

God, the Infinite, Divine, Eternal Beginning and the End, the Creator of all things, the Creator of time and space, who exists outside of time and space, takes to himself the nature of his creature. He gave birth to the sky and the earth, the oceans and the mountains - all with only a thought, and then he made himself into one conceived in a womb and born to a man and a woman, in a tiny village in a specific year within history. He did this to be an icon of himself for our sake and to unite himself to us in the deepest way possible in our human form.

God became one of us. The Creator of all things made Himself a creature. The Eternal Word became enfleshed. God took on human flesh.

Why?

God becomes man so that man might become God. He is madly in love with us. Our very existence came to be because His infinite and overflowing love couldn't be contained within the Trinity but it spilled out of Himself outwards, spreading to recreate itself in a form that could be received. He made us out of his own image so that we could experience the freedom necessary to make the choice to love Him out of that freedom, to share in His divine love. The human person is the satisfaction of God's infinite longing.

God is the satisfaction of every person's infinite longing. Infinite longing itself was created in us to draw us back to the Infinite.

We don't really get it. We don't really understand how human God made himself! Jesus was a human baby! He was a human infant, a human child. Jesus lay motionless, totally dependent on his parents to do everything for him, then he learned to crawl, and eventually to walk.

God nursed at the breast of a woman. God held the hand of his father to learn to walk. God felt all the feelings of human experience, from sadness and anger to humor and joy. He was hungry, full, tired, rested, enthusiastic and annoyed.

We also don't get how our humanity is made in His image. The longing for infinity we encounter within ourselves is the very imprint of God's own inner life stamped into our hearts.

There is so much of our human experience we would accept more willingly if we truly knew that God himself felt these things. It is too easy to dismiss uncomfortable or negative experiences as "bad" or "wrong," and many of us were raised to ignore, downplay, or repress certain facets of the human experience. Joseph and Mary taught Jesus how to grow into his full humanity. They affirmed him for who he was, a human boy, and raised him into a human man. By God's design, God made himself subject to this life - this family life - and in doing so sanctified it and made it divine. Jesus made it possible for Mary and Joseph to grow into the divine destiny of their full humanity. He opens that door for all of us.

"Joyful night of Bethlehem! The skies are opened; the earth trembles; the echoes of the universe repeat canticles of glory and of peace! 'Glory to God in high heaven, and peace on earth to men that are God's friends!' In the midst of the night when everything is silent, the omnipotent Word descends from His royal abode. There was a hush of silence all around, and night had but finished half her swift journey, when from Thy heavenly throne, Lord, down leaped the Word omnipotent. O wonderful exchange! God becomes man to make us Godlike. He becomes poor to make us rich. He shares our griefs to give us happiness! This marvelous exchange constitutes the basis of Christianity. It is the sublime thesis of Scripture. It is the divine drama of history because it is the mystery of Christ" (*Only Jesus, Luis Martinez*).

Reflection Questions:
What part of your humanity do you believe can't be from God? Sin is the misuse of our humanity, but what specific elements native to your humanity itself, maybe something in your personality, do you reject or find it hard to believe was willed by God to exist in your identity as a human person?

\\ WEEK 5 \\ KNOWLEDGE OF JESUS CHRIST
DAY 30: THE SACRED HEART

The infinite love which is the very being of God Himself, eternal and everlasting, that created the Heavens and the Earth, that was before all that is and will be forever long after everything we know has passed away, took the form of a human being and contained that love-beyond-all-description within the heart and spirit of that human. Jesus Christ, God-made-man, one with the Father and Holy Spirit who breathed creation itself into existence, contained within himself all the love that God consists of. This is the Sacred Heart. The heart of one man with true human nature inflamed with the infinite love of a Divine Person.

The devotion to the Sacred Heart of Jesus goes back to the revelations of Jesus to Saint Margaret Mary Alacoque in the 1690's. This is a life-changing and beautiful devotion to learn and practice. Jesus spoke to St. Margaret Mary and her words were recorded by Father John Croiset at the request of Jesus himself in her apparitions. The book in English is called *The Devotion to the Sacred Heart of Jesus* by Father John Croiset and should be picked up immediately.

Here is just one example devotional meditation from the book.

"Consider that the Sacred Heart of Jesus Christ was no sooner formed in the womb of the Blessed Virgin than It was inflamed with an immense love for all men; but, as it is the property of love to wish to be always with those loved, a life of thirty-three years appeared to Him too short to satisfy the ardent desire which He had to be always with us. In order to satisfy this greatest of all desires, He must perform the greatest of all miracles. The Sacred Heart could not place any limits to the excess of Its love. Be not afflicted, my apostles, said our loving Savior, if I am obliged to leave you to ascend to Heaven; My heart desires more ardently to be with you than you desire to be with Me, and as long as there will be men on this earth, I will be with them all days, even to the consummation of the world.

All the motives which had induced the Son of God to clothe Himself with our human nature had ceased; the work of the Redemption had been accomplished. It was the ardent desire of being always with us which induced Him to perform this continual miracle, the abridgment of all miracles by which His immense love put Him in a state of being no longer able to be separated from us. Jesus has ascended to His Father. Why does He return every day to this earth invisibly, if it is not because He cannot separate Himself from men and because His delights are to be with them? Could we have ever imagined that Jesus Christ would love us to this excess? It is from the highest pinnacle of His glory that He thinks of coming to lodge in our hearts, as if something were wanting to His happiness so long as He remained away from us. This desire must be very violent when it can continue to exist in Heaven, where all desires are satisfied. Jesus Christ must indeed love men passionately, since without being held back by the immense glory which He enjoys since His Ascension, He puts Himself daily in a humble and obscure state on our altars in order to satisfy the excess of this tender love, thus fulfilling what was spoken by the Prophet: 'My delights are to be with the children of men.' (Prov. 8:31)" (*The Devotion to the Sacred Heart of Jesus, p 258-259*).

Reflection Questions:
How much of your relationship with God is based on your experience of the passionate love Jesus feels for you? How much of your practice of religion is based on your experience of this love? What might be getting in the way of receiving this love?

\\ Week 5 \\ Knowledge of Jesus Christ
Day 31: The Eucharist

As Jesus is the Divine Person come to meet us in our humanity that we might commune with him and join together with him in union, the Eucharist is the manifestation of this desire that he remains with us until the end of the world. It is his infinite love that stretches beyond the limits of what is reasonable.

We grow up with stories of romance and adventure, heralding the great lovers who would go to great lengths to prove their love and be with their beloved. Thousand-mile journeys, endless discomforts, fire-breathing dragons guarding castles and imprisoned princesses - no problem for the great lover knight. We applaud those who risk their lives for the sake of their loved ones.

It takes a special kind of madness to conceive something so outrageous as to become food for one's beloved. It also takes Divine Power to be able to accomplish such a task. This is the madness of the love of God. He longs for union with us so deeply and doesn't want to wait for us to pass from this life to the next that he turns himself into our food that we may consume him and consummate our love with him.

"How sweet it was, the first kiss of Jesus to my soul! Yes, it was a kiss of Love. I felt I was loved, and I said, 'I love you, I give myself to you forever!' Jesus asked nothing of me, demanded no sacrifice. Already for a long time past, He and I had watched and understood one another... that day our meeting was no longer a simple look but a *fusion*. No longer were we two: I had disappeared as the drop of water which loses itself in the depths of the ocean, Jesus alone remained; the Master, the King!" (*Story of a Soul, Ch. 4*).

These thoughts of Saint Therese about the anticipation and participation of Holy Communion are like the private journal of a bride waiting for her wedding day. It is no surprise to find out the great mystic Saint John Paul II saw so clearly the marital embrace as the image of God's love for us. The marital embrace points to the reality of our consummation with God! It does so of course in a purely analogous way, but the imagery of Bride and Bridegroom, and God as Divine Lover fills the pages of Scripture.

We come back again to the quote from CS Lewis at the beginning of our consecration journey. We find in ourselves a longing for something infinite, that nothing in this world can satisfy. This longing points us to the reality of something beyond this world that can satisfy us. The love that waits for us is a Communion of Persons, so madly in love with us that They beckon us to Them even now. We are given faith by the Holy Spirit, to enter into communion with the Son by receiving Him into our bodies, and we unite to the Father in this Glory.

We must prepare our hearts and minds to receive Jesus in the Blessed Sacrament properly, just as St. Joseph was prepared to receive Jesus in the humble and hidden circumstances of Bethlehem. Mary was the tabernacle, the perfect earthly vessel that contained the Infinite Lover within her. Joseph was the first communicant, who received Jesus from this tabernacle and held him to his body.

Many people think history is a timeline that began at the Big Bang and continues until the Second Coming. History is instead a circle, radiating out from the center like ripples from a stone dropped into a pond. That disruption into the fabric of time and space is Jesus and that moment is the Incarnation. When God became Man at the Annunciation, time began. At that moment Mary and Joseph received the reality of Christ's presence into their marriage. It struck holy fear into Joseph's heart and holy abandonment as he said yes despite that fear. Can you imagine the awesome anticipation Joseph and Mary felt before the Nativity? God, the Infinite One, becomes a creature in space and time. The Divine Majesty hidden in a species that looks deceiving to anyone without faith.

Joseph held that baby knowing he was holding God.

Saint Joseph, help us receive Jesus in the Eucharist with the same anticipation and awe that you received him in Bethlehem. Even though he is hidden in a form that looks mundane to us, help us see with eyes of faith and behold the Glory of God, hidden for our sake. Help us consume him with the understanding that he descends from Heaven in each moment of consecration because of his infinite longing for us. Let us receive this immeasurable gift of the Divine Love Himself, and give ourselves to Him in return.

Reflection Questions:
What distortions of love in your past make it difficult to accept the fullness of God's plan for loving you? How can you prepare yourself to receive him in the Eucharist more faithfully, holding back nothing of yourself for yourself, so that He who gives himself completely to you may receive you completely?

\\ WEEK 5 \\ KNOWLEDGE OF JESUS CHRIST
DAY 32: THE CRUCIFIXION

Today we confront the greatest mystery of the Christian faith.

Jesus tells us in Matthew 6:25 to "not be anxious about your life." It is not a suggestion, or a hope- it is a command. He then goes on to explain that the birds and flowers are taken care of, because of the Father's love. The Father's love is key. If we believe the Father loves us, even more than the flowers and birds, then we can let go of "tomorrow's troubles." Do we trust this Father?

Saint Paul tells us "Be anxious for nothing, but in everything by prayer and supplication, with thanksgiving, let your requests be made known to God; and the peace of God, which surpasses all understanding, will guard your hearts and minds through Christ Jesus" *(Ph 4:6).*

Is this possible? This can be a very difficult point for many people, and probably one of the most common roadblocks to faith in Christ. "If God is good, all-powerful, and loves us, why does He let bad things happen to good people?"

When we experience that kind of pain, we immediately want it to go away. We think of everything possible to make it go away, and the thought that God, who could make it go away but doesn't, can be too difficult to bear. Therefore our minds come up with all kinds of arguments against God; either against his goodness, his power, his love, or his very existence. At times like these, it might make more sense to believe that God is angry, doesn't care about us, doesn't pay attention to us, or doesn't even exist.

Instead of asking, "Why, God?" we might ask instead, "Where are you, God?" Crying out to the Father, "Why have you abandoned me?" returns to us the faint echo of our words repeated in the mouth of Jesus who suffered with us. He felt it too. For our sake.

God did not save his own son from suffering. If He didn't do it when his own son cried out for him to "remove this cup" and cried out from the cross, "Why have you abandoned me?" there must be more to understand here. Why let his son and himself go through such suffering?

The answer can only be unrelenting love. God's love for us is why Jesus suffered the cross.

Here's a different way to understand suffering. Catholics are fond of the phrase, "offer it up" to try to encourage one another in the midst of suffering. There might be some validity to the sentiment, but it is also sort of misleading (and many times unhelpful). If you've ever been the one suffering and someone said, "offer it up," it may not have helped much. That's because "offer it up" has a sense of choice about it, as if you are choosing the suffering you are going through. We don't choose suffering; some suffering is forced upon us. Sometimes we suffer as a direct result of our choices, but even then, we certainly didn't choose the suffering part. Because of original sin, we suffer. Because of the world, our fallen nature, or spiritual temptation, we suffer - and not by choice.

The one who did have a choice was Jesus. He didn't have original sin, and he didn't have to suffer. The one who actually did have the freedom to "offer it up" is the one who didn't actually have to suffer.

Jesus, who did not have to suffer, chose to suffer because we suffer. **He looked at us, upon our crosses in life, and he said to himself, "If that's where you are, that's where I want to be."** He was like us in "all things but sin." This means he suffered everything we suffer. He suffered the heartache of losing friends, of loved ones dying, of being misunderstood, even of being overworked (trying to get away from the crowds for a little time to himself but being pulled back in because of people's needs). Ultimately, he even allowed himself to go through the excruciating pain of suffering all this without the consolation of God's presence. "My God, my God, why have you abandoned me?" Why did Jesus go through that? **Because we go through that.** He knew he wasn't going to take away our suffering, so he joined us in it. Where is God when we are suffering? He is with us, experiencing it all right by our side. That›s how we know we can trust him. He›s pursued us to the furthest ends of the earth - to the furthest extremes of human suffering - to be with us.

If you are tempted to doubt the goodness of the Father, maybe your doubt has more to do with the way you are thinking about it than the actual existence of the Creator of the Universe. Maybe there's a different way to see things in which, even in the midst of this earth's greatest tragedies, God is still Good.

Mary and Joseph

This is the disposition that Mary had, and we can imagine would have been the disposition of Saint Joseph. They joined their son in his suffering, also choosing it for our sake, and in doing so presented a perfect model of faith for us. The image of Michelangelo's *Pieta* shows us what this faith looks like. Mary, who raised the Son of God, witnessed countless miracles, hoped constantly in the salvation of the world through the Kingship of her son, then watched as he was beaten, crucified, and lay lifeless, dead in her arms. Joseph also had a share in this as he anticipated the suffering that lay ahead for his beloved wife and son. What tragedy can you imagine that could more powerfully test one's faith in the goodness of God? Mary held her dead son in her arms and still trusted God's goodness and his plan. Besides the agony in the garden, I can't imagine another moment in all of human history more complex with the spectrum of human emotion at the deepest levels.

"Now faith is the assurance of things hoped for, the conviction of things unseen" *(Hebrews 11:1)*. This is faith.

God is madly in love with us. He is our Father who loves us, who is trustworthy, the Divine Lover who wants to unite himself to us. He will take care of us, draw us to himself, and satisfy the deepest longing of our hearts- if only we trust Him and receive Him.

"Eros is that force within us which does not allow the lover to remain in himself, but it moves him to become one with the beloved. Eros is the stretching with every fiber of our body and soul for the fullness of love and life. Eros is the desire for the True, the Good, and the Beautiful. Eros is part of God's very heart. This is the passion, the fire, the love of the Bridegroom for the Bride. Jesus says "I thirst" because he is thirsting for us!

The Almighty awaits the yes of his creatures as a young bridegroom awaits the yes of his bride.

On the Cross, God's Eros is made manifest for us. Eros is indeed that force which does not allow the lover to remain in himself, but moves him to become one with the beloved. Is there madder eros than that which lead the Son of God to become one with us, even to the point of suffering as his own the consequences of our offenses?" (*Deus Caritas Est,* Pope Benedict XVI)

(These reflections are taken from Dr. Greg Bottaro's book *The Mindful Catholic.*)

Reflection Questions:
What hidden pain is holding you back? What have you suffered in your life that blocks you from the deepest level of trust and abandonment to God?

_____

_____

_____

_____

_____

_____

_____

_____

_____

_____

_____

_____

The Office of Readings for Holy Saturday contains a stirring reading from an "ancient homily."

"Something strange is happening - there is a great silence on earth today, a great silence and stillness. The whole earth keeps silence because the King is asleep. The earth trembled and is still because God has fallen asleep in the flesh and he has raised up all who have slept ever since the world began. God has died in the flesh and hell trembles with fear."

There is a psychological theory of brain and personality development called Attachment Theory. Part of the theory places importance on the experience of "ruptures" between baby and caregiver, which are then "repaired," giving the baby the sense that even when it seems there is no one else out there, someone always comes. Going to sleep is one of the first experiences of this rupture and repair. A baby learns that no matter how dark the night, dawn comes with the morning, and so does mom.

Imagine what it was like for Mary and Joseph to let Jesus go to sleep. They would almost have to go through their own rupture and repair, knowing they were in the presence of the Son of God, then letting him sleep! Over time it surely became easier, but first time parents who aren't caring for the Savior of the World can get a little anxious around the baby's safety while sleeping, so it would be fair to say that Mary and Joseph may have felt a little uneasy around this daily "loss."

I wonder if Mary recalled those moments as a new mom when she was holding her Son dead in her arms. What is happening? Will he be OK? Did God know what He was doing putting Jesus into our care?

Did Mary recall Joseph's strong presence as her husband and father of Jesus, reassuring her that everything was going to be alright? Did she pray to him at that moment? She sat in stillness and silence through Holy Saturday, the silence Joseph was so well known for. I imagine she called him to mind and asked for his presence and consolation that he offered her when he was alive.

The silence of Holy Saturday is a strange stillness that sharpens our attention on the movements of God. We know what is going to happen on Sunday, but Mary and Joseph did not have that benefit as they were living through these events in their lives. They had to trust God. They had to surrender to His holy will.

Jesus himself knew what to do in this strange silent stillness. It was the stillness of the Garden of Gethsemane. It was the torment of his heart, deeper than words, that expressed itself in blood sweat through his pores. It was the shocking, total, and utter acceptance of his human nature as he cried out, "Let this cup pass!" and then the acceptance of his divine Father as he said, "not my will but yours be done." He must have learned those words from his human father, who taught him how to sit in silence and encounter God in the prayer of the deep.

We feel this strange silence still today. When we walk into the church on Holy Saturday and see the Tabernacle door open, its contents gone, we know something is off. Where is Jesus?! Our spirits sink, twist, become unsettled. We awkwardly genuflect by accident, remembering halfway to the ground that we don't genuflect in front of empty boxes. Where is Jesus?!

The ancient homily answers:

"He has gone to search for our first parent, as for a lost sheep. Greatly desiring to visit those who live in darkness and in the shadow of death, he has gone to free from sorrow the captives Adam and Eve, he who is both God and the son of Eve. The Lord approached them bearing the cross, the weapon that had won him the victory. At the sight of him Adam, the first man he had created, struck his breast in terror and cried out to everyone: "My Lord be with you all." Christ answered him: "And with your spirit." He took him by the hand and raised him up, saying, 'Awake, O Sleeper, and rise from the dead, and Christ will give you light.'

'I am your God, who for your sake have become your son. Out of love for you and for your descendants I now by my own authority command all who are held in bondage to come forth, all who are in darkness to be enlightened, all who are sleeping to arise. I order you, O sleeper, to awake. I did not create you to be held a prisoner in hell. Rise from the dead, for I am the life of the dead. Rise up, work of my hands, you who were created in my image. Rise, let us leave this place, for you are in me and I am in you. together we form only one person and we cannot be separated.

'For your sake, I, your God, became your son; I, the Lord, took the form of a slave; I, whose home is above the heavens, descended to the earth and beneath the earth. For your sake, for the sake of man, I became like a man without help, free among the dead. For the sake of you, who left a garden, I was betrayed to the Jews in a garden, and I was crucified in a garden.

'See on my face the spit I received in order to restore to you the life I once breathed into you. See there the marks of the blows I received in order to refashion your warped nature in my image. On my back see the marks of the scourging I endured to remove the burden of sin that weighs upon your back. See my hands, nailed firmly to a tree, for you who once wickedly stretched out your hand to a tree.

'I slept on the cross and a sword pierced my side for you who slept in paradise and brought forth Eve from your side. My side has healed the pain in yours. My sleep will rouse you from your sleep in hell. The sword that pierced me has sheathed the sword that was turned against you.

'Rise, let us leave this place. The enemy led you out of the earthly paradise. I will not restore you to that paradise, but I will enthrone you in heaven. I forbade you the tree that was only a symbol of life, but see, I who am life itself am now one with you. I appointed cherubim to guard you as slaves are guarded, but now I make them worship you as God. The throne formed by cherubim awaits you, its bearers swift and eager. The bridal chamber is adorned, the banquet is ready, the eternal dwelling places are prepared, the treasure houses of all good things lie open. The kingdom of heaven has been prepared for you from all eternity." *(Office of Readings, Second Reading, Holy Saturday)*

This is where Jesus went while Mary held his lifeless body then laid it in the tomb. This is what he had to accomplish, and this is the reason we can trust God. Joseph's faith, Mary's faith, and Jesus's faith show us how to trust God in the face of all darkness.

Reflection Questions:
What doubt do we hold onto in our lives that we don't think God will take care of? It is easy to say we trust God, but do we act like it? What do we ruminate about? What do we stress about? What situations bring out the worst in us because we begin to feel the loss of control or worry that all will not be well?

\\ WEEK 5 \\ KNOWLEDGE OF JESUS CHRIST
DAY 34: THE RESURRECTION

It's interesting to note that the most important moments in life, and in history, happen in a moment. Often we carry the assumption that if something is really important, it must build up for a while, or unpack itself for a while. Creating a work of art may be like that. Working on some major project may seem like that. But even then, in the creative process or the project development, there is a moment. One single moment that means everything, where it all comes together, where it matters.

If we are not paying attention, those moments may completely pass us by. Parents know this as their children take a first step, speak a first word, or hit a first baseball. Moments may not feel so important to us as we are living through them, but anything that matters in life happened in a moment.

The moment of the tomb opening up, when Jesus Christ conquered death, is the moment that changes everything for all time. Because of the moment when Adam and Eve chose sin, and then the moment when Mary and Joseph said, "yes," we are lead to this moment. Jesus died for us. He hung on the cross and breathed his last breath as it was stolen from him because of the madness of his love for us. Ah He loves us so much! But that wasn't it.

The stone was rolled away, and Jesus was not there. The tomb was empty! This man, who loved so insanely that he suffered torture and death for the sake of his beloved, plummeted to the depths of death and came out alive.

The reason that this moment is so important is because it validates all the other moments that came before it.

There were many great and loving men in history. Some people are quick to point out that there have been many great spiritual leaders and think of Jesus as being in the company of Ghandi or Buddha, the Dalai Lama, or even Martin Luther King, Jr. It's easy to accept the "goodness" of Jesus when he's simply one of many great men.

Jesus is a little different though. He said a lot of great, loving things. He stood up for social justice and preached mercy and kindness. But at the same time, with just as much clarity, he preached the reality of hell. He could not have been clearer that our behaviors matter, and the choices we make in our life will be brought to us for judgment when we die. This is an incredibly uncomfortable reality. Especially in our modern culture, we don't like to think about being judged. We'd much rather think that we can be the masters of our own lives, make our lives what we want of them, and be judged on whether or not we were "nice to others."

We forget all too easily that Jesus is KING. Most of us in western culture don't have any idea what it's like to live under the rule of a king. Jesus is LORD. We are made to bend a knee and fall to the ground in the presence of our King and Lord. Do we know what that means?

Many are too quick to judge "Kingship" and "Lordship" according to the plentitude of bad examples in history. We think having a Lord means suffering under someone who "lords" his power over us. When we refuse to give Jesus the proper worship as due the King and Lord of the universe, we are ignoring everything he taught us about his kingdom. This King came to serve, not to be served.

This King also proved everything he said when he conquered death. The stone was rolled away, and the tomb was empty.

Jesus said unbearably controversial things. He said he was God. He said there was a hell that many would go to for their sins. He said he had the power to forgive sins, and he gave that power to his priests. He said he would die for our sins. He told his priests to offer up bread and wine to be transformed into his own body and blood. He said so many things that people thought were crazy when they heard it, that they walked away from him *despite the miracles that he was working in their very sight!* To the horror of the religious of his day, he said he would tear down the Temple and rebuild it in three days!

Then he did it. He offered himself up to death. He lay dead in his mother's arms. He was buried. Three days later, his body was not to be found. None of the other "great men" could conquer death. None of them are worth listening to the way Jesus is worth listening to. None of them are King and Lord of the universe, of all time, of all eternity.

Our God is madly in love with us. Oh how much He loves us! Despite how silly and adolescent we are in our pride, balking at his rightful authority, going against his will over and over again, he pursues us to the ends of the earth. He chases us down even to the darkest recesses of death to retrieve us. When we say Alleluia, we need to mean it! Alleluia! It's all true! The tomb was empty! Jesus is King! He is real and he is alive! And oh, how he loves us!

Reflection Questions:
What are you holding onto in your life that goes against the teaching of Jesus? What commandments do you have the most difficulty with? Where does the authority of the Church challenge you the most? Open it all up to Him today. Sing Alleluia with all the saints and angels of Heaven, proclaiming that you are in need of a Savior, and you have One!

\\ Week 5 \\ Knowledge of Jesus Christ
Day 35: Divine Mercy

In my experience, the single deepest wound in the hearts of those I treat in therapy has to do with being and worth. The truth is human beings are created out the image of God, molded in the form of Jesus in his humanity, formed with this mark of the Divine. This is what gives us value. We have it from the very moment of our conception. The existence of a unique DNA code signifying the existence of a new person is infinitely more valuable than the largest and most perfect diamond on earth.

This truth, however, needs to be taught to us by our parents or those who raise us when we are children, forming our first sense of self and identity. We are not typically given the perfect combination of attention and autonomy, love and limits that nurture this correct sense of self. Most of us grow up with the instability of the weakness of others, who respond to us unintentionally based on our actions instead of our being. We learn that it is what we do that makes us valuable, not who we are. We grow up feeling that if we could lose or gain more value based on our actions, there must not be any inherent value we possess based simply on our being.

This is diametrically opposed to the reality of our creation and what God wants us to know about ourselves. Our actions matter, but not the way we think. Jesus does not ask us to be perfect before we go to him. He does not expect us to be perfect before he will come to us. He is madly in love with us as we are! He offers this love to us, which is the only authentic reason to go to him, and that love perfects us.

This is the difference between a dad teaching us we are good, and we want to be good to live up to this identity, and a dad withholding his affection and validation until we've shown him that we are good. St. Joseph taught Jesus he was good as he was, who he was without having to do anything. The being of Jesus drew Joseph and Mary's contemplation, awe, and captivated love. You share that same humanity with Jesus. Your being should also draw contemplation, awe, and captivated love. Jesus is madly in love with you. You as you are, not you as you ought to be. Only in relationship with Jesus, receiving the love of God without deserving it, can you be transformed.

God has been teaching his people this message since He created Adam and Eve. There are great biblical studies that explore this story in great depth. (See Scott Hahn's book, *A Father Who Keeps His Promises*.) The New Testament flows from the Old Testament seamlessly, and Jesus is the full manifestation of this love of God. He did not stop 2000 years ago though. For centuries he has continued to unfold the intricate delicacies of his love for us.

We've already touched on the revelations of Jesus and his Sacred Heart to St. Margaret Mary Alacoque in the 17th Century. The unfolding of God's mercy in history continued with St. Therese of Lisieux in the 19th Century. (There are plenty of lesser known saints in between as well. For example, see Saint Teresa Margaret of the Sacred Heart from the 18th Century). The 20th Century brought us Saint Faustina and her *Diary of Divine Mercy*. It seems that with every new century, Jesus is making it clearer and clearer how radical his love and mercy is for us.

Because we think we have to be perfect before we can have a relationship with God, we miss out on what God's love is really all about.

Father Michael Gaitley, MIC says, "Jesus' Heart is particularly moved with compassion when he sees anguished souls stuck at the bottom of the rough stairway to perfection. His Heart absolutely breaks when he further sees so many of these souls falling into the pits of discouragement, despondency, and even despair. In fact, this situation has become too much for him. It's caused him to snap, once again. For this time, he does more than simply reveal his Heart, as he did to Saint Margaret Mary. This time the arms of his heartfelt compassion reach down to embrace such little souls and carry them to the heights of holiness, as he taught to Saint Therese." (*Consoling the Heart of Jesus*, 78).

Saint Therese taught the spirituality known as the "Little Way." In short, our weaknesses become our strengths. Think of two daughters who break something that belongs to their father. When he comes home one runs and hides because she fears him, and the other jumps into her father's arms with tears telling him how sorry she is. One daughter broke the father's heart, the other consoled it. Which do you think is which?

It turns out there are two ways to deny God's love and mercy. The first has to do with our pride, or maybe insecurity, feeling that we don't need to ask for forgiveness or submit ourselves to any higher authority. We like to imagine that we are in control. It makes us feel better to ignore our weakness and pretend that we have all the answers.

The second way to deny God's love and mercy can be a bit more insidious. We start with a recognition of our weakness and sin, which is a good thing, but then we feel that we are beyond that mercy of God. We believe we are too sinful, damaged to the core, unworthy of being in a close relationship with God. This happens often to people who are striving along the path of perfection, who submit themselves to God's authority, recognize their need for him, but then start to focus too much on their own imperfections. This is just another form of pride! This is what drove Judas to hang himself. If only Judas had given in to Christ's love, he would have been forgiven.

Saint John Paul II recognized this story unfolding in time and history and implemented the Sunday after Easter to be Divine Mercy Sunday. This is in direct recognition of the apparitions of Divine Mercy to St. Faustina, but really encompasses the unfolding of this beautiful love song that God is singing to us. He is serenading us, one century at a time. Take a break from your busy life, where you are either running away from your weakness by pretending to be in control, or running away from your weakness by trying to prove your worth, and listen to Jesus tell you that he is strong in your weakness, that he loves you in your weakness, to stop running away from your weakness. Let's stop this rumination for a moment and see if we can hear His song.

Reflection Questions:

Do you typically avoid your weakness by pretending you are in control, or feeling that you need to earn the strength of having worth? If the former, how can you submit yourself in one way today to the reality that you do not have the control you would like. If the latter, how can you submit yourself in one way today to the reality that God's love is bigger than your imperfection?

_____
_____
_____
_____
_____
_____
_____
_____
_____
_____
_____
_____
_____
_____
_____
_____
_____
_____
_____
_____
_____
_____
_____
_____
_____
_____
_____

Week 5 Prayers

Litany of the Holy Name of Jesus
Lord, *have mercy on us.*
Christ, *have mercy on us.*
Lord, *have mercy on us.*

Jesus, hear us. *Jesus, graciously hear us.*
God the Father of Heaven *Have mercy on us.*
God the Son, Redeemer of the world, *Have mercy on us.*
God the Holy Spirit, *Have mercy on us.*
Holy Trinity, one God, *Have mercy on us.*

Jesus, Son of the living God,   *Have mercy on us.*
Jesus, splendor of the Father,   ...
Jesus, brightness of eternal light.
Jesus, King of glory.Jesus, sun of justice.
Jesus, Son of the Virgin Mary.
Jesus, most amiable.Jesus, most admirable.
Jesus, the mighty God.
Jesus, Father of the world to come.
Jesus, angel of great counsel.
Jesus, most powerful.
Jesus, most patient.
Jesus, most obedient.
Jesus, meek and humble of heart.
Jesus, lover of chastity.
Jesus, lover of us.Jesus, God of peace.
Jesus, author of life.
Jesus, example of virtues.
Jesus, zealous lover of souls.
Jesus, our God.
Jesus, our refuge.
Jesus, father of the poor.
Jesus, treasure of the faithful.
Jesus, good Shepherd.
Jesus, true light.
Jesus, eternal wisdom.

Jesus, infinite goodness.
Jesus, our way and our life.
Jesus, joy of Angels.
Jesus, King of the Patriarchs.
Jesus, Master of the Apostles.
Jesus, teacher of the Evangelists.
Jesus, strength of Martyrs.
Jesus, light of Confessors.
Jesus, purity of Virgins.
Jesus, crown of Saints.

Be merciful, *spare us, O Jesus.*
Be merciful, *graciously hear us, O Jesus.*

From all evil,   *deliver us, O Jesus.* (after each line)
From all sin,   *deliver us, O Jesus.*
From Your wrath,   ...
From the snares of the devil. ...
From the spirit of fornication.
From everlasting death.
From the neglect of Your inspirations.
By the mystery of Your holy Incarnation.
By Your Nativity.
By Your Infancy.
By Your most divine Life.
By Your labors.
By Your agony and passion.
By Your cross and dereliction.
By Your sufferings.
By Your death and burial.
By Your Resurrection.
By Your Ascension.
By Your institution of the most Holy Eucharist.
By Your joys.
By Your glory.

Lamb of God, who takes away the sins of the world,
spare us, O Jesus.

Lamb of God, who takes away the sins of the world,
graciously hear us, O Jesus.
Lamb of God, who take away the sins of the world,
have mercy on us, O Jesus.

Jesus, hear us.
Jesus, graciously hear us.

Lord Jesus Christ, You have said, "Ask and you shall receive, seek, and you shall find, knock, and it shall be opened to you." Grant, we beg of You, to us who ask it, the gift of Your most divine love, that we may ever love You with our whole heart, in word and deed, and never cease praising You.

Give us, Lord, as much a lasting fear as a lasting love of Your Holy Name, for You, who live and are King for ever and ever, never fail to govern those whom You have solidly established in Your love. Amen.

\\ WEEK 6 \\ KNOWLEDGE OF THE HOLY FAMILY
DAY 36: POOR IN SPIRIT

> "Blessed are the poor in spirit,
> for theirs is the kingdom of heaven.
> Blessed are those who mourn,
> for they shall be comforted."
> *(Matthew 5: 3-4)*

For our final full week of preparation for the Consecration to Jesus through Saint Joseph, we're going to reflect on the Holy Family and specifically in these next four days, how they are a family of the Beatitudes.

There are few things more American than self-reliance. Our country was formed with the belief of independence and the "can do" ideals (meaning "**I** can do."). We swim in a culture that tells us not to rely on anyone but ourselves. This pool of self-reliance teaches us that weakness or poverty is not only unattractive, but something to be avoided or hidden at all costs. "Never show your enemy your weakness." This mentality is so pervasive that we don't even know that this is actually the exact opposite way of life that Jesus in the Gospels teaches us. He tells us that those who are truly poor - detached from the things of the world - are not only blessed, but that they will inherit the kingdom of heaven. They are the truly rich!

Being truly poor in spirit means that any illusions we have of ourselves are stripped away. Over time and healing grace from the Father, we can begin to see ourselves as we truly are. The Holy Family had no illusions about themselves. They knew exactly who they were. They lived in complete confidence that Jesus was the Son of God, Mary was the Mother of God, and Joseph was the guardian and protector of the Holy Family. Each of them was a beloved daughter or son of the Father. Living from that place of humble confidence and the truth of their identities, they were free to truly give themselves to the other and truly free to receive the gift of the other. They understood that the little they had was a total gift from the Father and that all they desired was to be given over to Him.

"The experience of poverty is meant to help us realize what we truly have in our hearts, to know ourselves as we are, without illusions. It is meant also to awaken a new hunger in our hearts, hunger for God. In poverty at the heart of the struggle, we realize that no food, no satisfaction, and no human security can suffice. We must direct our desires toward God" *(Father Jacques Philippe, The Eight Doors of the Kingdom, 38).*

If we spend time meditating on the hidden life of the Holy Family, we might ask, "what was it like to live in the same house as the Immaculate Heart of Mary, the Sacred Heart of Jesus, and the Most Chaste Heart of Joseph?" Can you imagine the intimate and consoling things shared between the Three Hearts? As they shared those most beautiful things, they felt the depth of the joy and love in all of God's creation of which we only get a glimpse. We can imagine that they experienced a deeper sorrow for fallen humanity, because they understood the cosmic reverberations of human frailty. In this mourning for humanity, the Holy Family found consolation in each other and in God. "To be consoled means realizing that our experience, bad as it seems, is really a precious good. It means giving thanks" *(Father Jacques Philippe, The Eight Doors of the Kingdom, 98).* They opened up their sorrowful hearts in trust that God will bring good out of all things.

Reflection Questions:
Can you see your weakness and poverty as a gift? As something lovable to the Father? What keeps you from experiencing and living the confidence that you are loved by the Father in your poverty? Is it difficult to trust in the Lord's providence in times of sorrow? Do you believe He desires to console you? And that He will?

"Blessed are the meek, for they share inherit the earth.
Blessed are those who hunger and thirst for righteousness,
for they shall be satisfied."
(Matthew 5: 5-6)

We've all had those moments when someone innocently says something that sets us off - it could be a co-worker or spouse or friend or family member - and before you know it, we've opened our mouths and something not-so-nice comes out. The moment we've lashed out, a wave of guilt washes over us, and we instantly regret our response. When we bring this to the Lord, He can show us that our lashing out may be a sign of our own need for healing, that we have a sensitivity to a particular wound that is still open and in need of care. Why did I respond with such anger? What's underneath all of that? How can I keep from lashing out?

One could say that growing in meekness can help us to find healing. Meekness is not a lack of emotion or passion. Meekness is not cold. A person striving for meekness is someone who is humble and willing to look at their poverty and weaknesses; someone who isn't afraid to enter into those places in their heart, with the Lord, that are in need of healing. The Holy Family lived a life of meekness. They lived a hidden life in Nazareth, unnoticed by those around them. The Immaculate Mary and the Son of God lived in a village and no one knew! They were approachable and down to earth, unassuming and unpretentious... they were meek, but they were far from cold. Think of the passion that ran through their hearts and their home! Passion for the salvation of souls, passion for defending humanity from the work of the evil one, passion for each person that crossed their path ... but no one knew.

When we encounter the hardness in our own hearts - those places in need of healing - the encounter with the meekness of Jesus can heal us. "Only intimate contact with the heart of Jesus can heal the hardness of the human heart" *(Father Jacques Philippe, The*

Eight Doors of the Kingdom, 105). When we open those hardened places in our heart to Jesus, His love and mercy will soften us ... will heal us ... will teach us how to live passionate meekness, like the Holy Family.

This desire for healing and the willingness to let the Lord into those places in our heart is the thirst for justice. "The thirst for justice is a thirst for conversion, for interior transformation"*(Father Jacques Philippe, The Eight Doors of the Kingdom, 132).* It is a thirst for holiness and wholeness. It is a desire for the places we have been wronged by others and where we have wronged others to be made right, to be healed. It is a thirst for union and communion with the Lord.

The passion of the Holy Family was a hunger, a thirst, and a longing for all to be made right. It was a longing for us to be in union and communion with God, within ourselves, with each other, and with all of creation. This passion, this thirst, this hunger, this longing of the Holy Family was a manifestation of God' thirst for us. "There is a thirst more ardent that all human desire. I mean God's thirst, the thirst of Jesus himself. God thirsts to love us and give himself to us ... God' desire to love us can never diminish or be extinguished ... God will always want to love us, to give himself to us, to save us ... We must believe that God wants to wed us in spite of our ugliness and, believing, allow him to do it. It is he whose gaze will make us worthy and clothe us in beauty. If we let ourselves be visited by and wed to the Lord, he will make us part of his thirst" *(Father Jacques Philippe, The Eight Doors of the Kingdom, 136-137).*

Reflection Questions:
Where are the places in your heart that you feel a need for deeper healing? In a time of prayer, with the Holy Family by your side, ask the Father to reveal the places in your heart that He thirsts to heal.

_____

_____

_____

_____

_____

\\ WEEK 6 \\ KNOWLEDGE OF THE HOLY FAMILY
DAY 38: MERCIFUL

"Blessed are the merciful, for they shall obtain mercy.
Blessed are the pure in heart, for they shall see God."
(Matthew 5:7-8)

We all need mercy. We need it probably more than we realize. We've been praying litanies during this consecration and we've prayed the words, "Have mercy on us" many times. Praying those words is meant to be a reminder to us of our daily need for mercy. We long for the Lord to see the woundedness of our lives and our hearts and beg Him not to give us what we truly may deserve, but to look upon us with His Heart and give us mercy. "In Latin, mercy is signified by 'misericordia.' This is two words combined, the Latin 'miseriae' meaning misery and the Latin 'cor' or 'cordis' meaning heart. It is the nature of God's mercy that His heart extends into our misery and redeems it. ... Mercy signifies that God draws our misery into His own infinitely loving heart." (Steven Jonathan Rummelsburg, *Misericordia: The Roots of Mercy*, 2015) When God draws our misery into His Heart, our sin, our mistakes, our wounds are burned up in the fire of His Mercy.

Our encounter with the Lord's mercy is what enables us to GIVE mercy and forgiveness to others who have hurt us. It is the grace we need to forgive and to pray for those who have hurt us. "It is not in our power not to feel or to forget an offense; but the heart that offers itself to the Holy Spirit turns injury into compassion and purifies the memory in transforming the hurt into intercession" *(Catechism of the Catholic Church, 2843)*. One of Our Lady's titles that we pray in the Hail Holy Queen is "Mother of Mercy." Jesus IS mercy itself. The Holy Family literally lived with the Heart of Mercy. Jesus learned the gift of mercy in the Holy Family and He spoke that longing to forgive those who wronged Him when He cried out on the cross, "Father forgive them, for they know not what they do" *(Luke 23:34)*.

"Purity of heart finds expression in mercy. Mercy purifies hearts as nothing else does" *(Father Jacques Philippe, The Eight Doors of the Kingdom, 177)*. Some stop at purity of heart and think it only speaks of chastity and sexual purity. It is that, but it is so much more! To have a pure heart means that your whole self is oriented to God - your thoughts, your actions, your words, all of you - and with that purity of heart, you begin to see everything around you as God sees. You begin to see the person in front of you as God sees and you act in a way that honors the gift of God in each person. "Purity is above all a matter of orientation; toward what and whom are my hope, my prayer, my desire directed? Nothing purifies the heart so much as praising and blessing God. A grateful heart is a pure heart" *(Father Jacques Philippe, The Eight Doors of the Kingdom, 173)*.

In the Holy Family lived the most pure hearts in creation... the Immaculate Heart, the Sacred Heart, and the Most Chaste Heart of Saint Joseph. Each heart was oriented to the Lord. Each heart found its hope in God. Each heart directed its desires and prayer to God. May the Three Hearts helps us to live purely. "A pure-hearted person has truly chosen to believe fully in God, hope fully in him, and love him with all his or her heart" *(Father Jacques Philippe, The Eight Doors of the Kingdom, 172)*.

Reflection Questions:
Where are the places in your heart in need of the Lord's mercy? As the consecration draws near, it would be a good time to begin to plan to receive the Sacrament of Reconciliation (Mercy!) before the consecration date. Spend time this week, using these reflections as a examination of conscience to prepare for the Sacrament. Always remember to hold the hands of mercy when looking at your sin and weakness. Is my life oriented to God? Are my thoughts, actions, and desires given over to the Lord for purification?

_____

_____

_____

_____

_____

\\ WEEK 6 \\ KNOWLEDGE OF THE HOLY FAMILY
DAY 39: PEACEMAKERS

"Blessed are the peacemakers,
for they shall be called the children of God.
Blessed are those who are persecuted
for the sake of righteousness,
for theirs is the kingdom of heaven."
(Matthew 5:9-10)

Have you ever gazed upon the face of a sleeping child and was amazed at how peaceful they looked? Not a care in the world or an anxiety in their heart. Did your heart long for such peace and contentment? From where does the peace of a child, not just in sleep, come? It comes from the place in their heart where they have complete confidence that they are safe, that they are cared for, and that someone they love will defend them. It comes from experiencing their identity as children of loving and caring parents. They have no need for worry. They have total confidence and are at peace. This is the peace that our hearts long to live in, but what along life's journey steals our peace? Often it comes from having wounded parents who let us down, who didn't keep us safe, or who didn't know how to love us as we were created to be loved. How can we find the healing and the peace for which our hearts long?

"... peace does not come from outside, from the world. It comes from our communion in faith and love with Jesus, the Prince of Peace. It is a fruit of prayer. God is an ocean of peace, and it is in intimate union with him through prayer that our hearts find peace" *(Father Jacques Philippe, The Eight Doors of the Kingdom, 186-187).* The gift of the Holy Family living this beatitude of peace and union with God is that they want to offer this beatitude - this peace - to each of us. For the ways that your mother and father failed to love you, Mary and Joseph deeply desire to love you in the way you needed to be loved. They long to have you enter into their family and to live as adoptive sons and daughters of the Holy Family. We are heirs to the Holy Family - children of God!

149

When we live with peace and confidence in our identity as sons and daughters of the Holy Family and of the Father, we can have peace in the midst of persecution. We've all had our faith and our beliefs misunderstood or ridiculed by our families, friends, or co-workers. In those moments of persecution, what is our response to be? Is it to confront them with how wrong they are? Are we called to persecute them, too? Somehow Jesus tells us that we are "blessed" in our persecution. We are blessed for being misunderstood. How can this be? It can be this way, because to be persecuted is to follow in the footsteps of Jesus, Himself.

Being persecuted for the sake of righteousness is to be persecuted, because we are living in the righteousness of God. This IS a blessing. We are called to respond to persecution just as Jesus did. We are called to have complete confidence that as sons and daughters of the Father, He will protect us. He will make right and good come from this persecution, whether it is for ourselves or for others. Enduring persecution increases our capacity to trust the Father. It increases our capacity to be union with the suffering and persecuted Christ.

As we close our reflections on the Holy Family as the Family of Beatitude, I wanted to share a final thought from Father Jacques Philippe on how Our Lady lived the Beatitudes perfectly. I'd suggest that as you read it, you read it in light of the meditations so far, and in the light of St. Joseph as well. Can we not say that the Holy Family - as a communion of persons - lived the Beatitudes perfectly?

"Mary lived each of the Beatitudes perfectly, and she helps us understand and practice them effectively...Through her we shall become poor in heart, humble and meek; in her arms we shall be consoled, she will make us hungry and thirsty for God, will make us good and merciful, will share with us the purity of her heart, will establish us in a profound peace to be shared with those around us. She will give us the grace of being strong in the combat and embracing the Cross as a grace. She will open wide the gates of the Kingdom and of true happiness" (*Father Jacques Philippe, The Eight Doors of the Kingdom, 213-214*).

Reflection Questions:

What are areas of your life that are not in peace? What are the places in your heart that are in need of healing and peace? Spend time with Our Lady and Saint Joseph, sharing those places with them. Open your heart to let them love you there. Do you have confidence in your identity as a beloved daughter or son of the Father? How might receiving your true identity help you in times of adversity?

> "We may say that the Holy Family was a
> Trinity on earth, which in a certain way represented
> the Heavenly Trinity Itself."
> ~ *St. Francis de Sales*

Before this reflection begins, it must be said that there is no way to gain direct experience of anything of God 's actual being through anything of this earth. The Trinity Itself is infinitely beyond anything we can even imagine. Yet, God does want us to know Him, and he gives us the ability to draw further into the depth of his mystery by way of analogy, reflection, and prayer.

You may be familiar with St. John Paul II's work, *Theology of the Body*. He breaks down in this series of teachings the way God imprinted the image of the Holy Trinity into humanity - more specifically into the bodies of man and woman, their relationship, and the offspring they bear. In the Book of Genesis God says, "Let us make man in our image." Note the "us." God is speaking from His Trinitarian voice even in the first book of Scripture. Out of this image, "Male and female He created them." Genesis brings us immediately into this awareness that somehow the creation of man and woman together can point us to the Holy Trinity.

The connection can be understood as such: In man we see the initiator of the gift of physical life. The seed that will unite with its complement begins in him, and he makes a gift of his very self in the act of sending forth this seed, this gift of life. The gift is received by the woman, who takes it into herself, unites it to part of herself, and nurtures it there. A child is the fruition of the gift and receptivity of gift. The man is drawn to the woman out of love, and he gives himself to her because of love. The child is the fruit of love, the fruit of two persons giving and receiving each other.

This dynamic of self-gift leads our minds and hearts closer to contemplating the reality of the Trinity. God the Father is the initiator of the gift. Jesus the Son receives the gift and in return, is a gift to His Father. The love that eternally spirates between and from the two of them is the third person of the Trinity, the eternal and infinite Fruition of Love between the Father and Son, the Holy Spirit.

The basis for the comparison between a human family and the Divine Trinity is the capacity for self-gift. The very love we have been reflecting on all along, the love that is the curriculum in the School of Love of the Holy Family, is the very love that the Divine Trinity consists of.

The Trinity is the Divine perfection of infinite and eternal self-gift and love. The love between Joseph and Mary is the perfection of human self-gift and love. The fruit of their love is also at the same time the fruit of the love between Mary and the Holy Spirit, which is the self-gift between what is human and Divine.

If Jesus was perfect in his humanity as he was in his Divinity, he was the fruit of the perfect love of a perfect mother and father. As Jesus consisted of every perfection, in both his humanity and in his Divinity, his very being pronounces the perfection of the love of his human parents.

Joseph, Mary, and Jesus, then are the perfect human image of the Holy Trinity. Not only are they the image, but they are the gate. They are the passageway through which we all enter into communion with the Holy Trinity. Through our Baptism we are adopted by Mary and Joseph, who take us into the embrace of their perfect school of love, united to Jesus, and through that union we are united to the Father by the power of the Holy Spirit.

All of creation was ordered to the creation of man and woman, which means that all of creation pointed to Jesus from the first moment of creation, which means that all creation, flowing from the Trinity, pointed to the Holy Family, the image of the Trinity, from the first moment of creation. Joseph, Mary, and Jesus stand at the center of space and time, and history flows outwards from their existence.

Reflection Questions:

How is your love imperfect? Who are you called to make the greatest gift of self to in your particular vocation? How can you give a little more of yourself today than you did yesterday to be faithful to who you are called to love?

_____
_____
_____
_____
_____
_____
_____
_____
_____
_____
_____
_____
_____
_____
_____
_____
_____
_____
_____
_____
_____
_____
_____
_____
_____
_____
_____
_____
_____
_____
_____
_____
_____
_____

\\ WEEK 6 \\ KNOWLEDGE OF THE HOLY FAMILY
DAY 41: INSTRUMENT OF SALVATION

Today's reflection is taken mostly from *Redemptoris Custos*, the Apostolic Exhortation of St. John Paul II that we have often been quoting from. As we draw closer to the day of consecration, we go deeper into the mystery of Jesus Christ revealed to us through the Holy Family. These passages warrant slow, prayerful, and repeated reading.

"It pleased God, in his goodness and wisdom, to reveal himself and to make known the mystery of his will *(cf. Eph 1:9)*. His will was that men should have access to the Father, through Christ, the Word made flesh, in the Holy Spirit, and become sharers in the divine nature *(cf. Eph 2:18; 2 Pt 1 4)*..."

In other words, as St. Athanasius said, "The Son of God became man so that we may become God" *(The Incarnation of the Word, 54,3)*.

"Together with Mary, Joseph is the first guardian of this divine mystery. Together with Mary, and in relation to Mary, he shares in this final phase of God's self-revelation in Christ and he does so from the very beginning." (5)

"Joseph's way of faith was totally determined by the same mystery, of which he, together with Mary, had been the first guardian. The Incarnation and Redemption constitute an organic and indissoluble unity, in which 'the plan of revelation is realized by words and deeds which are intrinsically bound up with each other.' Precisely because of this unity, Pope John XXIII, who had a great devotion to Saint Joseph, directed that Joseph's name be inserted in the Roman Canon of the Mass-which is the perpetual memorial of redemption - after the name of Mary and before the apostles, popes and martyrs." (6)

As we have been reflecting on throughout this preparation, Joseph was an integral element of the Incarnation as the husband of Mary.

Here we see that salvation itself is "organically and indissolubly" united to the Incarnation, and therefore also to the total gifts of self made by Joseph and Mary.

"Saint Joseph was called by God to serve the person and mission of Jesus directly through the exercise of his fatherhood. It is precisely in this way that, as the Church's Liturgy teaches, he 'cooperated in the fullness of time in the great mystery of salvation' and is truly a 'minister of salvation.' His fatherhood is expressed concretely 'in his having made his life a service, a sacrifice to the mystery of the Incarnation and to the redemptive mission connected with it; in having used the legal authority which was his over the Holy Family in order to make a total gift of self, of his life and work; in having turned his human vocation to domestic love into a superhuman oblation of self, an oblation of his heart and all his abilities into love placed at the service of the Messiah growing up in his house.'" (8)

"The Gospels clearly describe the fatherly responsibility of Joseph toward Jesus. For salvation-which comes through the humanity of Jesus-is realized in actions which are an everyday part of family life, in keeping with that 'condescension' which is inherent in the economy of the Incarnation." (8)

This is truly remarkable. The beauty, wonder, and awe of this sentence is unending. "Salvation is realized in actions which are an everyday part of family life."

"Salvation is realized in actions which are an everyday part of family life."

SALVATION IS REALIZED IN ACTIONS WHICH ARE AN EVERYDAY PART OF FAMILY LIFE.

"The communion of life between Joseph and Jesus leads us to consider once again the mystery of the Incarnation, precisely in reference to the humanity of Jesus as the efficacious instrument of his divinity for the purpose of sanctifying man: 'By virtue of his divinity, Christ's human actions were salvific for us, causing grace within us, either by merit or by a certain efficacy...'"

"If through Christ's humanity this love shone on all mankind, the first beneficiaries were undoubtedly those whom the divine will had most intimately associated with itself: Mary, the Mother of Jesus, and Joseph, his presumed father..."

"Why should the 'fatherly' love of Joseph not have had an influence upon the 'filial' love of Jesus? And vice versa why should the 'filial' love of Jesus not have had an influence upon the 'fatherly' love of Joseph, thus leading to a further deepening of their unique relationship? Those souls most sensitive to the impulses of divine love have rightly seen in Joseph a brilliant example of the interior life." (27)

Joseph formed Jesus, and Jesus formed Joseph. God became man so that we might become God.

Reflection Question:
What everyday part of your family life needs to be purified so as to become more like acts appropriate to salvation?

_____
_____
_____
_____
_____
_____
_____
_____
_____
_____
_____
_____
_____
_____
_____
_____

As we come to a close on our general reflections of the Holy Family and near the end of the preparation in general, it is critically important to understand that we have not been reflecting on the virtue and greatness of Joseph, Mary, and Jesus to hold them up on a pedestal in silent adoration without the realization that it is our destiny as well. We hold them up, not as objects of awe alone, but as models to live our lives by. In their humanity, the Holy Family exemplifies the life of perfection that we are all called to live in our humanity. Not only do they exemplify it, but they facilitate it, opening up the channels of grace through the Incarnation and Resurrection that make it possible for us to join to their blessed happiness.

"This bond of charity was the core of the Holy Family's life, first in the poverty of Bethlehem, then in their exile in Egypt, and later in the house of Nazareth. The Church deeply venerates this Family, and proposes it as the model of all families. Inserted directly in the mystery of the Incarnation, the Family of Nazareth has its own special mystery" (*Redemptoris Custos, 21*).

We are not made to transcend our humanity in order to reach holiness in this life. It is impossible to rise above the core nature of our humanity to become something other than human. We are not made to be angels, or some weird humanized form of angelic-like distortion that many people assume holiness to look like. As we reflected on yesterday, "Salvation is realized in actions which are an everyday part of family life." The path Jesus opened up for us to go to Divine Union is the path through normal, everyday, human life.

"What is crucially important here is the sanctification of daily life, a sanctification which each person must acquire according to his or her own state, and one which can be promoted according to a model accessible to all people: 'St. Joseph is the model of those humble ones that Christianity raises up to great destinies;...he is the proof that in order to be a good and genuine follower of Christ, there is no need of great things - it is enough to have the common, simple and human virtues, but they need to be true and authentic'" (*Redemptoris Custos, 25*).

The "common, simple and human virtues" need to be "true and authentic." This is where we get into trouble. We all have an idea of what holiness is supposed to look like, and we are really good at convincing ourselves and others that we are measuring up to this superficial standard. It takes a deeper authenticity to accept the true path to holiness. It is not one of great and lofty and widely visible things. The Holy Family exemplifies for us a life of poverty, simplicity, and complete anonymity. The people close to them laughed at the idea that Jesus was anyone special. "Is this not the carpenter's son? The son of Mary?" We can hear their cynicism and scoff rolling off the page.

This is almost too much to bear. It was too much for the religious leaders of Jesus' time to bear. It was too much for the religious faithful of his day to bear. Jesus was too simple. Messiah? Blasphemy.

The Holy Family is a model of holiness for us and a reachable one. We must travail the arduous path of dying to self, letting go of our attachments to our false idols of superficial holiness that only end up serving our own pride. We must then be willing to do the actually difficult work of growing in charity in the context of "everyday family life." It's easy to feed the poor at a soup kitchen, it's much more difficult to feed your spouse and children with consistent words of kindness instead of impatience.

Reflection Questions:
Can we accept what the Holy Family models for us? What deeper areas of growth are you really in need of?

WEEK 6 PRAYERS

Seven Sorrows and Joys of Saint Joseph
(Recite one Our Father, Hail Mary, and Glory Be after each number)

1. St. Joseph, chaste spouse of the Holy Mother of God, by the sorrow with which your heart was pierced at the thought of a cruel separation from Mary, and by the deep joy that you felt when the angel revealed to you the ineffable mystery of the Incarnation, obtain for us from Jesus and Mary, the grace of surmounting all anxiety. Win for us from the Adorable Heart of Jesus the unspeakable peace of which He is the Eternal Source.

2. St. Joseph, Father of Jesus, by the bitter sorrow which your heart experienced in seeing the child Jesus lying in a manger, and by the joy which you felt in seeing the wise men recognize and adore Him as their God, obtain by your prayers that our heart, purified by your protection, may become a living crib, where the Savior of the world may receive and bless our homage.

3. St. Joseph, by the sorrow with which your heart was pierced at the sight of the Blood which flowed from the Infant Jesus in the Circumcision, and by the joy that inundated thy soul at your privilege of imposing the sacred and mysterious Name of Jesus, obtain for us that the merits of this Precious Blood may be applied to our souls, and that the Divine Name of Jesus may be engraved forever in our hearts.

4. St. Joseph, by the sorrow when the Lord declared that the soul of Mary would be pierced with a sword of sorrow, and by your joy when holy Simeon added that the Divine Infant was to be the resurrection of many, obtain for us the grace to have compassion on the sorrows of Mary, and share in the salvation which Jesus brought to the earth.

5. St. Joseph, by your sorrow when told to fly into Egypt, and by your joy in seeing the idols overthrown at the arrival of the living God, grant that no idol of earthly affection may any longer occupy

our hearts, but being like you entirely devoted to the service of Jesus and Mary, we may live and happily die for them alone.

6. St. Joseph, by the sorrow of your heart caused by the fear of the tyrant Archelaus and by the joy in sharing the company of Jesus and Mary at Nazareth, obtain for us, that disengaged from all fear, we may enjoy the peace of a good conscience and may live in security, in union with Jesus and Mary, experiencing the effect of your salutary assistance at the hour of our death.

7. St. Joseph, by the bitter sorrow with which the loss of the child Jesus crushed your heart, and by the holy joy which inundated your soul in recovering your treasure on entering the Temple, we beg you not to permit us to lose our Savior Jesus by sin. Yet, should this misfortune befall us, grant that we may share your eagerness in seeking Him, and obtain for us the grace to find Him again, ready to show us His great mercy, especially at the hour of death; so that we may pass from this life to enjoy His presence in heaven, there to sing with you His divine mercies forever.

Let us pray: God, who in your ineffable Providence has chosen Blessed Joseph to be the spouse of your most holy Mother; grant, we beseech you, that we may deserve to have him for our intercessor in heaven whom on earth we venerate as our holy protector: Who lives and reigns forever and ever. Amen.

\\ CONSECRATION PREPARATION \\
DAY 43: MAKING READY YOUR HEART AND MIND

Let us reflect on where we have come from and where we are going.

We recognized our attachments to broken ways of understanding love. At the root of sin is doubt in the goodness of God's plan for our lives, and we need teachers who show us the way. If we were not formed with perfect examples of total trust, full surrender, and limitless self-sacrifice, we suffer from a miseducation in love.

All of our wounds are taken on by Jesus, who unites us to himself in Baptism, and draws us away from our imperfection towards his perfection. This is a process of becoming, as we journey further into the fullness of the humanity we were created to express, day after day, year after year.

The fruit of this union is adoption through Jesus to becoming a child of, and one with, the Father, but we enter this union through our humanity and therefore become an adopted child of Joseph and Mary. We are here and now in that process of transformation - the healing process of conversion as we leave behind our broken doubtfulness and the attachment to our limited way of understanding what is good for us. In this new identity in Jesus we have Joseph as a father and Mary as a mother.

Mary nurtures us in her motherhood and Joseph leads and protects us in his fatherhood. We have dwelled in this reality for the last 43 days, drinking in the truths taught in this school of love. We let the healing waters of grace flow as we enter with hearts and minds into our true identities. Joseph leads the way, exemplifying the perfection of our humanity, and facilitates the entrance of God into our humanity so that union may be possible.

During this week one should go to confession and renounce sin with greater sorrow than ever before, having understood more deeply the dignity of our true calling, and with intention to live with purity and virtue in the way of Saint Joseph.

Sit with the words of Jesus to St. Faustina regarding confession: "When you go to confession, to this fountain of my mercy, the blood and water which came forth from my heart always flows down upon your soul and ennobles it. Every time you go to confession, immerse yourself in my mercy, with great trust, so that I may pour the bounty of my grace upon your soul. When you approach the confessional, know this, that I myself am waiting there for you. I am only hidden by the priest, but I myself act in your soul. Here the misery of the soul meets the God of mercy. Tell souls that from this fountain of mercy souls draw graces solely with the vessel of trust. If their trust is great, there is no limit to my generosity. The torrents of grace inundate humble souls. The proud remain always in poverty and misery, because my grace turns away from them to humble souls" (*Divine Mercy In My Soul*).

Then one should receive Communion in this state of grace, and receive Jesus in his body, blood, soul, and divinity with spirit and mind reflecting on how Joseph received Jesus in that moment of his appearance in our world at the Nativity.

The next step is to make the act of consecration. This is an intentional devotion, which is a form of perfect renewal of our Baptismal Vows. If you can't make it to Confession and Mass on May 1, the consecration may be made anyway, in celebration of the Feast of Saint Joseph the Worker, in accordance with our preparation. It can then be recited/renewed again after having confessed and received Jesus in the recommended way.

From this moment forward you will be led by Saint Joseph in a new way. Entrust yourself to him. Place yourself in his presence often and ask him to take care of you whatever your needs are as a child would ask of a father. Have confidence in this as Jesus could never be disturbed by greater trust, devotion, and affection for his own earthly father. He takes it as a form of devotion to himself as you draw closer to him in union.

Reflection Questions:
What do you hope for as a fruit of this consecration? What intention do you have to place trustingly in the hands of your father, Saint Joseph?

_____
_____
_____
_____
_____
_____
_____
_____
_____
_____
_____
_____
_____
_____
_____
_____
_____
_____
_____
_____
_____
_____
_____
_____
_____
_____
_____
_____
_____
_____
_____
_____
_____
_____
_____

DAY 43 PRAYERS

Come Holy Spirit
Come, Holy Spirit, fill the hearts of your faithful and enkindle in them the fire of your love.

Send forth your Spirit and they shall be created.And you shall renew the face of the earth.

Let us pray. O God, who by the light of the Holy Spirit, did instruct the hearts of the faithful, grant us in the same Spirit to be truly wise and ever to rejoice in His consolation. Through Christ our Lord.
Amen.

Magnificat
My soul proclaims the greatness of the Lord,
my spirit rejoices in God my Savior;
for he has looked with favor on his lowly servant.
From this day all generations will call me blessed:
the Almighty has done great things for me,
and holy is his Name.

He has mercy on those who fear him
in every generation.
He has shown the strength of his arm,
he has scattered the proud in their conceit.
He has cast down the mighty from their thrones,
and has lifted up the lowly.
He has filled the hungry with good things,
and the rich he has sent away empty.
He has come to the help of his servant Israelfor he has
remembered his promise of mercy,
the promise he made to our fathers,
to Abraham and his children forever.

DAY 44: CONSECRATION

Today's the day! If you haven't already, get to confession this week in honor of your consecration. Receive communion in the spirit of Saint Joseph's receptivity of Jesus, and if possible, recite this consecration in front of the Blessed Sacrament.

In the name of the Father, the Son, and the Holy Spirit:

Mary, blessed virgin, mother of God and my mother, be with me now as I ask for the intercession of your husband. Holy Spirit, pour Yourself into my heart that I may feel the warmth of God's love and know His care and protection. Draw me deeper into the Most Sacred Heart of Jesus that I may be transformed by Love into Love itself, in union with the Father. Heavenly Father, be with me now as I seek to unite myself more deeply than ever before to you especially through the intercession and example of your representative of perfect fatherhood on earth, St. Joseph.

Saint Joseph, during these forty-four days, I have prepared my heart to know you more intimately and to grow in my desire to consecrate my life and my heart to Jesus through your intercession. I place myself in your hands as I make this consecration.

Through this preparation, I have sought to know my identity as a beloved child of the Father. I have witnessed your fatherhood to Jesus as an image of the Fatherhood of God. I ask your help to learn my true identity from your love and to live out of it each day.

Saint Joseph, man of virtue, you are a witness to me of true humility, generosity, and love. Help me to grow each day in the virtues I need to live my identity to the fullest. Help me to have the clarity to see which imperfections I need to work on. Help me to have the humility to seek the Sacrament of Reconciliation when I fall short and encourage me to keep striving for holiness.

Saint Joseph, you and the Blessed Virgin Mary lived your lives in complete trust in the Father's providence for you. I ask for your help to always give my fiat, my yes, to the Father's will. Help me to always place all of my decisions in the light of God's will. Help me to trust Him entirely with all that I have and all that I am.

Saint Joseph, you are a model for me of silence, purity, and humility. Your silence and humility show me your receptivity to the Father's will. Your purity shows me honor for myself and others in my thoughts and actions. I ask for your help to honor myself, others, and the Father's will in my life. Pure Heart of Joseph, help me to see God in myself, in others, and in Himself.

Saint Joseph, you desire to lead me to intimacy with Jesus Christ. Your witness to Him shows me what a life of trustful surrender and mercy looks like. I ask for your help to surrender my life and my heart to the love and mercy of Jesus Christ. As you raised him on earth, raise him once again in me. Form him in me, and me in him.

You lead the Holy Family in Beatitude. I ask for your help to grow in poverty of spirit, meekness, mercy, and purity. Help me to embrace the Trinity living within me through my baptism.

On this day _____, I _____ a repentant sinner and beloved child of the Father renew and ratify the vows of my baptism. I renounce Satan and all attachment to sin. Saint Joseph, I consecrate myself this day to Jesus Christ through your intercession. I commit myself to Jesus Christ and desire to follow Him more closely. I consecrate all that I am and all that I have to Jesus Christ and ask your intercession to live my life in accord with His love and mercy. May you and your Holy Family guide and protect my heart and my life. May I grow in holiness and virtue after your example. May I be ever more willing to die to self, to seek only the Lord's Will and may my life be a witness to your trusting and humble heart. Saint Joseph, Most Chaste Heart, make my heart like yours. Saint Joseph, pray for me.

In the name of the Father, the Son, and the Holy Spirit, Amen.

Have you enjoyed this book?

If so, please check out more of the work of the **CatholicPsych Institute**, which promotes the full integration of the human person through the study of faith and psychology, as well as the mission of the **Theology of the Body Institute.**

www.catholicpsych.com

www.tobinstitute.org

And if you haven't joined our Facebook Group yet, you can find us under "Saint Joseph Consecration."

Saint Joseph – PRAY FOR US!